Lecture Notes in Computer Science   11461

More information about this series at http://www.springer.com/series/7411

Benoît Hilt · Marion Berbineau ·
Alexey Vinel · Magnus Jonsson ·
Alain Pirovano (Eds.)

Communication Technologies for Vehicles

14th International Workshop
Nets4Cars/Nets4Trains/Nets4Aircraft 2019
Colmar, France, May 16–17, 2019
Proceedings

 Springer

Editors
Benoît Hilt
University of Haute Alsace
Mulhouse, Colmar, France

Alexey Vinel
Halmstad University
Halmstad, Sweden

Alain Pirovano
École Nationale de l'Aviation Civile
Toulouse, France

Marion Berbineau
French Institute of Science
and Technology, Spatial Planning,
Development, and Networks
Villeneuve d'Ascq, France

Magnus Jonsson
Halmstad University
Halmstad, Sweden

ISSN 0302-9743   ISSN 1611-3349 (electronic)
Lecture Notes in Computer Science
ISBN 978-3-030-25528-2   ISBN 978-3-030-25529-9 (eBook)
https://doi.org/10.1007/978-3-030-25529-9

LNCS Sublibrary: SL5 – Computer Communication Networks and Telecommunications

This Springer imprint is published by the registered company Springer Nature Switzerland AG
The registered company address is: Gewerbestrasse 11, 6330 Cham, Switzerland

Preface

The Communication Technologies for Vehicles Workshop series provides an international forum on the latest technologies and research in the field of intra- and inter-vehicules communications. This workshop is organized annually to present original research results in areas related to the physical layer, communication protocols and standards, mobility and traffic models, experimental and field operational testing, and performance analysis.

First launched by Tsutomu Tsuboi, Alexey Vinel, and Frei Liu in Saint Petersburg, Russia (2009), the workshop has been held in Newcastle-upon-Tyne, UK (2010), Oberpfaffenhofen, Germany (2011), Vilnius, Lithuania (2012), Villeneuve d'Ascq, France (2013), Offenburg, Germany (2014 Spring), Saint Petersburg, Russia (2014 Fall), Sousse, Tunisia (2015), San Sebastiàn, Spain (2016), Toulouse, France (2017), and Madrid, Spain (2018). These proceedings gather the papers presented at the 14th edition of the workshop, which took place in Colmar, France, in May 2019. The workshop was supported by the University of Haute Alsace, IRIMAS Institute and with the technical support of the IFSTTAR, France, and Halmstad University, Sweden.

The call of papers resulted in 15 submissions. Each of them was assigned to the Technical Program Committee members and ten submissions were accepted for publication. Each paper had three reviewers. The order of the papers in these proceedings corresponds to the workshop program. This year the keynote speakers were:

- Pr. Falko Dressler, "Cooperative Automated Driving: From Assistance Systems to Networking to Human Interaction," Universität Paderborn, Paderborn, Germany
- Pr. Serge Chaumette, "Myriads of *Nets: Understanding and Addressing the Issues of Constrained and Possibly Hostile Environments," University of Bordeaux/LaBRI, Talence, France
- Virginie Taillandier, "Carrefour Intelligent or Smart Level Crossing," SNCF, Paris, France

We extend a sincere "thank you" to all the authors who submitted the results of their recent works and to all members of the Technical Programm Committee.

May 2019

Benoît Hilt
Marion Berbineau
Alexey Vinel
Magnus Jonsson
Alain Pirovano

Organization

Nets4Workshop 2019 was organized by the Department of Computer Science, University of Haute Alsace, Colmar, France.

Executive Committee

General Co-chairs

Marion Berbineau	IFSTTAR, France
Benoît Hilt	University of Haute Alsace, France
Alexey Vinel	Halmstad University, Sweden

TPC Co-chairs

Sébastien Bindel	University of Haute Alsace, France
Frédéric Drouhin	University of Haute Alsace, France
Alain Pirovano	ENAC, France

Web Chair

Frédéric Drouhin	University of Haute Alsace, France

Publication Chair

Sébastien Bindel	University of Haute Alsace, France

Steering Committee

Marion Berbineau	IFSTTAR, France
Sébastien Bindel	University of Haute Alsace, France
Frédéric Drouhin	University of Haute Alsace, France
Benoît Hilt	University of Haute Alsace, France
Alain Pirovano	ENAC, France
Alexey Vinel	Halmstad University, Sweden

Technical Program Committee

Wahabou Abdou	University of Burgundy, France
Marion Berbineau	IFSTTAR, France
Gérard Chalhoub	University Clermont Auvergne, France
Hacene Fouchal	University of Reims, France
Antonio Freitas	University Clermont Auvergne, France
Marc Gilg	University of Haute Alsace, France
David Matolak	University of South Carolina, USA

Juan Moreno Garcia-Loygorri	Universidad Politécnica de Madrid, Spain
Alain Pirovano	ENAC, France
Thomas Sprösser	University of Haute Alsace, France
Dorine Tabary	University of Haute Alsace, France

Co-organizing Institutions

Halmstad University, Sweden
IFSTTAR, France
University of Haute Alsace, France

Sponsoring Institutions

City of Colmar, France
IRIMAS Institute, France
University of Haute Alsace, France

Contents

Rail

Road

Towards a 5G Vehicular Architecture

Léo Mendiboure[1]([✉]), Mohamed Aymen Chalouf[2], and Francine Krief[3]

[1] LaBRI Lab, University of Bordeaux, Bordeaux, France
`leo.mendiboure@labri.fr`
[2] IRISA Lab, University of Rennes 1, Lannion, France
[3] LaBRI Lab, Bordeaux INP, Bordeaux, France

Abstract. In the coming years, the vehicular networks should be integrated in a global 5G network. Indeed, the 5G system aims to respond to a wide range of services including Ultra-Reliable and Low-Latency Communications (URLLC) and, therefore, vehicular communications. However, the current Cooperative-Intelligent Transport Systems (C-ITS) architecture does not meet the key design recommendations of the 5G architecture design. Thus, this integration is not possible yet. Indeed, five different improvements should be considered to make it possible: network intelligence and automation, edge data processing and interoperability, network control, environment virtualization and finally security and privacy. Different papers have already proposed architectures enabling some of these improvements through the integration of different technologies in the C-ITS architecture. To highlight their strengths and their limits, these states-of-the-art solutions are compared. None of them propose a solution meeting the five identified improvements. That is why this paper presents a new architecture taking all these improvements into account. In particular, to complete the existing work, automation, security, privacy and trust are considered. To do so, a knowledge plane enhancing the functioning of the whole architecture is designed. Moreover, a security and privacy plane, strengthening trust in the vehicular environment thanks to Blockchain, is proposed. The role of the different components of this four-plane architecture is also described. Finally, some of the main challenges of the deployment of the proposed architecture are discussed.

Keywords: IoV · C-ITS · 5G · AI · NFV · SDN · Blockchain

1 Introduction

The vehicular networks and the Intelligent Transport Systems (ITS) are constantly evolving. Recently, a new paradigm emerged, the Internet of Vehicles (IoV), a combination of the vehicular ad-hoc networks and the vehicles telematics connecting vehicles, humans and things. In the future, these vehicular networks should be integrated in a global 5G network. Indeed, the 5G system aims to respond to a wide range of services including enhanced Mobile BroadBand (eMBB), massive Machine Type Communications (mMTC), Ultra-Reliable and

B. Hilt et al. (Eds.): Nets4Cars/Nets4Trains/Nets4Aircraft 2019, LNCS 11461, pp. 3–15, 2019.
https://doi.org/10.1007/978-3-030-25529-9_1

Low-Latency Communications (URLLC) and, therefore, vehicular communications. Based on the network slicing idea, this system (5G) should be able to provide a high Quality of Service (throughput, latency, reliability, etc.) meeting the requirements of the different types of applications and services.

Different standardization bodies are working on an ITS standardized architecture: the European Telecommunications Standards Institute (ETSI) in Europe, the International Standard Organization (ISO) and the Association for Radio Industry and Business (ARIB) in Japan and the Institute of Electrical and Electronic Engineers (IEEE) in the USA. Through the joined efforts of these standardization bodies, an ITS reference architecture emerged. This architecture, the first release of the Cooperative-ITS architecture (C-ITS), is shown in Fig. 1 and specified in ETSI 302 665 [6] and ISO 27217. This architecture aims to provide road safety, traffic efficiency and comfort services in the vehicular environment. It is composed of three main planes. The first one is the management plane operating the network, the applications and the architecture. The second plane is the control plane ensuring the data processing and transmission. This plane is composed of four layers: access technologies, networking and transport, facilities and applications. Finally, the last plane is the security plane providing security services such as authentication, confidentiality and profile management.

However, the integration of this C-ITS architecture in the 5G system is not yet possible. In fact, this architecture does not meet the key design recommendations of the 5G architecture identified by the 5G-PPP group [8]. Indeed, this architecture presents many limitations as shown in [10]: processing and storage capabilities for handling global information, guarantees of QoS, interoperability, adaptability to the growing vehicular traffic and guarantees of privacy and security for the users. Therefore, to be integrated in the 5G system, it should evolve towards a more flexible, programmable, secured and intelligent system. To meet the 5G design recommendations, five different points should be considered: network intelligence and automation, edge data processing and interoperability, network control, environment virtualization and, security, privacy and trust.

Most of these features correspond to different technologies and techniques forming the basis of the 5G system. For example, Software Defined Networking (SDN), decoupling the network control plane and data plane, could improve the dynamicity of the network control with programmability. Similarly, Network Function Virtualization (NFV), facilitating the virtualization of the network functions, could be used to reduce cost and design a more flexible and modular architecture. Artificial Intelligence (AI) techniques should enable a higher level of automation of the network, optimizing operating performances. Finally, Edge Computing (EC) and Big Data Analysis (BDA) could provide storage and computational capabilities at the edge of the network. It could enable a local and optimized data management and processing improving the applications performances, the user experience and the core network offloading.

As these technologies are identified, different papers have already proposed to enhance the different planes of the C-ITS architecture using EC, AI, SDN, NFV or the combination of these different technologies. These propositions are presented and compared in Sect. 2 of this paper. However, to the best of our knowledge, none of these papers propose a global solution meeting the five identified requirements: security, control, virtualization, data processing and automation. Therefore this paper aims to go further than the existing work by proposing an evolution of the C-ITS architecture tackling these five requirements and, in particular, improving security, privacy and automation. To do so, a four-plane architecture, completing the three-plane C-ITS reference architecture, is designed. Two innovative ideas are introduced: a knowledge plane improving the whole network operating and a security and privacy plane strengthening trust using Blockchain (BC). Moreover, the role of the components of the four planes are described and the main challenges of this architecture are discussed.

The rest of this paper is organized as follows: Sect. 2 compares the state-of-the-art solutions enhancing the C-ITS architecture while Sect. 3 introduces a new architecture meeting the identified requirements. Finally, the main challenges related to the deployment of this architecture are tackled in Sect. 4.

2   Related Work

The C-ITS reference architecture, proposed by the standardization bodies (ISO, IEEE, ETSI, etc.), is the starting point for most research activities. To improve the vehicular communications, the integration of different components in the three-plane model shown in Fig. 1 have been proposed. In this section are compared different papers tackling the five key areas of work we identified: network intelligence and automation, edge data management, network control, environment virtualization and security and privacy. Moreover, we highlight the limits of these proposals to explain why a new architecture should be proposed.

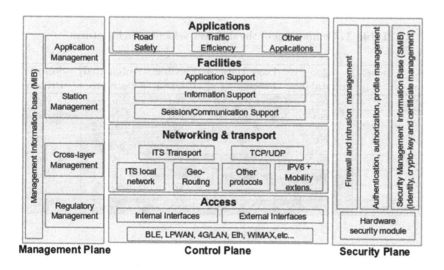

Fig. 1. C-ITS reference architecture

2.1   State-of-the-Art Solutions

The future vehicular networks should inter-connect humans, things and vehicles. Therefore, interoperability and data processing are among the most important challenges. That is why the authors of [10] modified the third layer of the control plane of the C-ITS reference architecture (Facilities Layer). This layer, renamed Artificial Intelligence layer, stores, processes and analyses the data produced by the lower layers. Thanks to that, the applications operation is optimized and the interoperability enabled. To do so, this layer is based on different techniques including Vehicular Cloud Computing (VCC), BDA and Expert System. The authors also introduce a fifth layer, the Business layer, at the top of the control plane. Using statistical analysis of the uses of the vehicular applications, this layer could improve the vehicular networks adoption and commercialization. However this paper only focuses on one of the five points identified, data processing, and does not introduce the idea of edge data processing.

The work described in [4] also focuses on interoperability, data management and data exchange. The authors propose a control plane composed of seven layers: user interaction, acquisition, pre-processing, communication, management and business. According to them, the deployment of this architecture could result in three main benefits: interconnection of devices to heterogeneous networks, quick integration of new communication technologies, and improvement of the applications operation. These authors also consider security as a major concern in this paper and in [3]. However the defined security plane is based on the existing standardized protocols (C2C Security Management Information Base, CALM Hardware Security Module, etc.). Thus, no solution is proposed to overcome the limitations identified in [3]: scalable and reliable authentication and access control mechanism and privacy preserving approach. Moreover in these papers the ideas of QoS, control and automation are not tackled.

Table 1. Comparison of the different vehicular architectures

Prop. \ Benef.	QoS Adaptability	Edge Data Processing	Flexible Control	Automated Decisions	Security Privacy
[10]	No	Cloud process.	No	NoNo	No
[4], [3]	No	Cloud process.	No	No	Identification
[9]	No	No	Yes	Only for control	No
[1]	No	Yes	Yes	No	No
[2]	Yes	Mentioned	Mentioned	No	No
[11]	Yes	No	No	No	No
Proposition	Yes	Yes	Yes	Yes	Yes

To deal with the network heterogeneity, the vehicular mobility and the increasing vehicular traffic, a flexible and scalable network control is a real asset.

That is why a Software Defined vehicular architecture (SD-IoV) is defined in [9]. This paper focuses on a SDN-based control plane and data plane. In this context, the "networking and transport" layer is controlled by a distributed hierarchical architecture of SDN controllers. Using a knowledge plane, the controllers could be used for data pre-processing, network analysis and feedback functionalities. The authors also introduce the idea of an infrastructure layer (or access layer) decomposed into two sub-layers: upper (switches and wireless access infrastructure) and lower (vehicles) data planes. As this paper focuses on the control plane, the issues of QoS, security and data processing are not addressed.

While [4] and [10] mainly focus on data processing and interoperability, they did not address the issues of QoS (latency) and efficiency. That is why the authors of [1] improved the five layer architecture introduced in [10]. To do so, they proposed to integrate Fog Computing capabilities at the Artificial Intelligence layer. It could extend the cloud computing capabilities to the edge of the network. Thanks to that, the location of the data processing could be optimized, the response time could be reduced and the network core could be off-loaded. This paper also presents a two level SDN control. In fact, a central SDN controller could be deployed within the management plane. This controller would be responsible of the definition of policies. Similarly, secondary SDN controllers could be deployed within the control plane, at the AI layer (fog resources management) and at the "networking and transport" layer (network devices management). In this paper, solutions are introduced for only two of the five identified issues: edge data processing and dynamic control.

With the IoV and 5G paradigms, the vehicles will be connected to everything (V2X). Different use cases, with different QoS requirements, can be imagined. To best meet their requirements, a flexible and reliable architecture should be designed. NFV and network slicing should be the key enablers. On the basis of four key performance indicators (communication type, latency, data rate, reliability), the authors of [2] suggest a classification of the vehicular services into five main categories. These categories are: safety and traffic efficiency, autonomous driving, tele-operated driving, vehicular internet and infotainment and remote diagnostics and management. This work also examines the benefits of network slicing at the RAN level, at the CN level and at the user device level. Finally, this paper proposes a management and orchestration of the autonomous driving slice based on the ETSI NFV standard and presents an architecture integrating edge computing. Similarly, the work presented in [11] applies network slicing for 5G-V2X services. Indeed, slicing the network into two categories: autonomous driving and infotainment, the authors propose an implementation and an evaluation of network slicing. This relevant study demonstrates the benefits of integrating network slicing in the vehicular architecture. Nevertheless, the control, automation, security and processing limitations are put aside.

2.2   Positioning

These different papers propose some improvements of the C-ITS reference architecture. In fact, the questions of QoS adaptability [2,11], edge data processing

[1,2,4,10] and flexible control [1,2,9] are discussed. However, they do not meet all the identified requirements (Table 1). In addition, two main points have not been addressed yet: automation, on the one hand, and security and privacy, on the other hand. Indeed, even if the authors of [4] identify security and privacy as an important issue, no solutions are envisaged. Similarly, a decision-making process based on a knowledge plane is suggested in [9] but is not described and should only be used by the SDN control plane.

That is why, in this paper, we introduce a new architecture extending the existing work. This architecture tackles the issues of Qos adaptability, edge data processing and flexible control but also focuses on automation and security and privacy. Indeed, an independent knowledge plane, improving the architecture functioning, and a security and privacy plane, enabling trust establishment using the Blockchain technology, are proposed.

3   Towards a Four-Plane Architecture

In this section, we present our four-plane architecture designed to enable the integration of the vehicular networks in the 5G system. To achieve this, this architecture tackles the five challenges that we identified: QoS adaptability, edge data processing, control flexibility, automation and security and privacy. The first sub-section presents an overview of the architecture while the other sub-sections provide details on the different planes forming it.

3.1   Overview

Figure 2 shows the proposed architecture that could be considered as an evolution of the C-ITS reference architecture. Unlike the previous propositions, this architecture is composed of four planes: the Management and Orchestration Plane (MOP), the Knowledge Plane (KP), the Control and Data Plane (CDP) and the Security and Privacy Plane (SPP). Thanks to this structure, the vehicular networks could be more flexible, dynamic, secured, efficient and automated. In this architecture, each plane has a specific role to play:

– the MOP is responsible of the global management of the architecture. Indeed, in a virtualized environment based on the idea of network slicing, handling the different network slices is a key point [2]. The MOP should be able to individually operate these slices and the services providers attached to them, to manage the interaction between these network slices, to define global management policies and to administer the physical infrastructure;
– the KP aims to improve the functioning of the other planes. Indeed, it will be able to retrieve, process, analyse data from the different planes (MOP, CDP, SPP) and make decisions. Using AI techniques and a shared knowledge database, the security and privacy, the network control, the resources positioning and the network management could be automated and optimized;

- the CDP is responsible of data processing and network control and operation. It is composed of five different layers: perception layer (PL), network and transport layer (NTL), facilities layer (FL), application layer (AL) and business layer (BL). Each of these layers has a specific function: data retrieval through sensors (PL), data transport (NTL), data storage and processing (FL), services definition (AL) and business models definition (BL);
- the SPP should be able to provide security, data protection and privacy preserving services to the different planes of the architecture (MOP, KP, CDP). Indeed, different types of services should be ensured by this plane: authentication at different levels, authorizations management and access control, profile management, firewalling, intrusion detection, user privacy, etc.

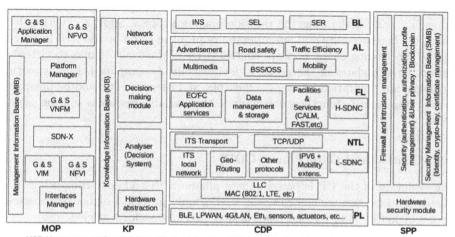

MOP: Management and Operation Plane; KP: Knowledge Plane; CDP: Control and Data Plane; SPP: Security and Privacy Plane
BL: Business Layer; AL: Application Layer; FL: Facilities Layer; NTL: Network and Transport Layer; PL: Perception Layer

Fig. 2. A four-plane architecture for the vehicular networks

3.2   Management and Orchestration Plane (MOP)

The improvement of the MOP is mainly based on two different technologies: Network Function Virtualization (NFV) and Software Defined Networking (SDN). Indeed, to provide customised and isolated services with different QoS requirements (latency, bandwidth, etc.) [2], a virtualized infrastructure seems to be the ideal solution. For example, reliable and low latency communications for the safety applications could be guaranteed.

With the integration of NFV and SDN, different components are integrated in the original MOP. These components should be used within each Slice (corresponding to S in Fig. 2), but should also be used to Globally manage the slices as a whole (corresponding to G in Fig. 2). The first of them is the NFV Infrastructure (NFVI) corresponding to the virtualization layer and the hardware and virtualized resources of the system. These resources are allocated to the virtual network functions by the Virtual Infrastructure Manager (VIM). The lifecycle of these functions is managed by the Virtual Network Functions Manager (VNFM). At a upper level, the global management of the CDP is ensured by the SDN-X, a central controller defining data management policies. For its part, the NFV Orchestrator (NFVO) manages the whole NFV infrastructure and the software resources. Finally, the Application Manager is the Application Programming Interface (API) of the MOP. It is used by the other planes and by the service providers to interact with this system.

With these technologies, the network services provided by legacy devices are replaced by virtualized softwares. This virtualization layer could be useful for the KP. Indeed, standardized data could be provided, simplifying data retrieval, enhancing and accelerating the decision-making process. Similarly, with softwares, the heterogeneity and interoperability problem could be resolved improving the functioning of the network control (CDP). Moreover, thanks to virtualization, large updates of the network devices could be simplified. Finally, with virtualization, migration becomes achievable, and therefore, it could be possible to move the security functions according to the available resources and the users needs.

3.3   Control and Data Plane (CDP)

The evolution of the CP is based on two pillars: SDN and edge computing [1]. Thanks to these two technologies, the CDP should provide a higher responsiveness, a higher dynamicity and more flexible and value-added services.

As it is shown in [5], edge computing, deployed at the Facilities Layer, may reduce delays, improve context-awareness and flexibility and off-load the core network. Indeed, pre-processing data at the edge could significantly reduce the network traffic. Similarly, if applications were deployed at the edge, for example multimedia applications (Augmented Reality), it might be possible to design low latency, high responsiveness and context-aware applications improving the user Quality of Experience. That is why the integration of this technology in the vehicular architecture is really promising.

With SDN, a dynamic network control could be designed. Indeed, SDN separates the network control and data planes and enables programmability. Therefore, the network can be re-configured on the fly. That is why the SDN controllers could be useful at two levels: the Network and Transport Layer and the Facilities Layer. For example, at the Facilities layer, during the rush hours, the network could easily be re-configured: the load could be balanced between different servers and new servers could be dynamically deployed. It may also be possible to interconnect cloud and edge servers, to enable interoperability between edge devices or to move virtual machines according to users needs. SDN could also be useful at the Network and Transport Layer to control the SDN switches: static nodes and mobile nodes. Indeed, with SDN, the hardware is abstracted and heterogeneous devices may be easily interconnected. Finally, the packets, depending on their importance (safety applications for example), could be prioritized.

As well as optimizing the CP, SDN could also be useful for the other planes. Indeed, a SDN controller can modify the behavior of the network devices: adding or removing forwarding rules. Therefore, the SPP could be improved by quick and easy deployment of firewalls or global intrusion detection systems. Moreover, SDN acts as an abstraction layer, and could provide large volumes of data to the Knowledge Plane, improving the data analysis process. Finally, as SDN is also integrated in the Management and Orchestration Plane, it is also a tool serving the management and orchestration actions.

3.4 Security and Privacy Plane (SPP)

Despite the standardized security protocols (WAVE IEEE 1609.2, S-IC C2C, CALM S-MI & HSW) designed for the vehicular environment, there are still open issues [3]. Some of the security and privacy challenges in IoV are directly related to the vehicular features: high mobility, topology, number of vehicles, heterogeneity, etc. To adapt security to this environment, scalable systems enabling intrusion prevention, authentication, privacy preserving and, especially, trust establishment are necessary. Moreover, some other problems are related to the integration of open source technologies in the architecture: SDN, NFV, etc.

To face these different challenges, we have to propose a solution which should be flexible, scalable, distributed, reliable and able to manage heterogeneous devices. As we have suggested in [13], Blockchain (BC), a popular distributed ledger technology could be the basis of this solution. Blockchain aims to provide a scalable, secured and trustworthy system without a trusted central authority [14]. Using Blockchain in vehicular environment, the main security functions that could be ensured are: authentication, integrity, confidentiality, availability, access control and non repudiation and, also, privacy, anonymity and trust.

For the MOP, with NFV, the network functions will be virtualized and their configuration and management should be secured. Therefore, solutions should be imagined and the Blockchain technology could be a key enabler. Within the CDP, security, privacy and trust are necessary at the different levels. Indeed, both the applications, the SDN controllers and the vehicles should be identified. As we proposed in [13], a Blockchain-based framework could be developed to authenticate and to control the behavior of the different nodes. Thanks to that, trust could be established in a mobile and heterogeneous environment. Finally, as the KP provide services which could be used by the different planes and different applications, access control is required. Blockchain-based access control solutions are currently being developed and could be integrated in this architecture.

3.5 Knowledge Plane (KP)

The Knowledge Plane is a widespread view and for the mobile ad hoc networks, the definition of such a plane has already been presented in [12]. However it has not been proposed yet in the vehicular architecture. This KP could provide many benefits in this environment, including, network automation and automatic pilot, decision-making aid, smart orchestration or cost reduction.

This KP is based on different components shown in Fig. 2. The first one is the Knowledge Information Base (KIB) corresponding to one or several databases containing information generated by the other planes of the architecture: MOP, CDP and SPP. At the same level, the Hardware Abstraction module can also be found. This module should be used as an abstraction layer enabling the retrieval of data in a standardized format. At an upper level, the Analyser is responsible of data processing and data reduction, extracting useful information from a large amount of data. Thanks to that, the Decision-making module should be able to make decisions and to propose corrections or optimization automating the decision-making process. Finally, the Network services is the Application Programming Interface (API) of the KP. Through this module, the other planes should be able to retrieve useful information or to optimize their functioning. Using AI techniques (Machine Learning, Deep Learning, neural networks), this KP could process and generate data and rules, correcting, improving, optimizing, controlling or validating the behavior of the other planes.

Automation is an important challenge for the MOP. Indeed, many tasks could be improved with AI and a global KP: optimization of the placement of the network functions, applications and resources, correction of the orchestrator errors (malfunctions), definition of policies, etc. For the SPP, data analysis could be useful to identify normal and abnormal packets. In fact, security could be enhanced by AI. For example, intrusion detection systems could be based on the KP. Finally, this plane could have many benefits for the CDP: cross layers decisions, handover management, dynamic network behavior management, packet prioritization if an abnormal situation is identified, etc.

4   Challenges

The different components introduced in this paper aim to improve the performances of the vehicular networks to design a 5G-compatible vehicular architecture. This architecture should be more flexible, dynamic, secured and automated. However, it is based on different technologies: NFV, SDN and edge computing. The integration in the vehicular architecture of these technologies is not without challenges. That is why, in the next sub-sections, the major challenges related to this integration are presented for each plane: MOP, CDP, SDPP and KP.

4.1   Management and Orchestration Plane (MOP)

For the MOP, there are two kinds of challenges. On the one hand, the NFV technology still have some limitations to overcome. For example, the reliability of the NFV Orchestrator is a significant problem and there still have open challenges in this field [7]. Moreover, the performances (latency, bandwidth, power consumption) of the Virtual Network Functions should also be considered. On the other hand, in the vehicular environment, many points should be considered: a standardized definition of the network slices and use cases, a definition of the exchanges between these slices and the urbanization of the architecture with an optimal positioning of the different functions, applications and resources.

4.2   Control and Data Plane (CDP)

In [9], is proposed an interesting architecture based on SDN and different challenges are identified, mainly, resource abstraction and network intelligence. Indeed, the SDN integration raises questions. In fact, it is important to determine whether or not this approach could be used for safety applications: algorithms based on this technology should be developed and their performances assessed in a real environment. The edge computing paradigm also brings some challenges. Indeed, different edge computing solutions have been developed and their inter-operability is currently an issue. Moreover, for these technologies [5], different problems should be tackled: scalability and mobility (Cloudlet), tasks scheduling (Fog Computing) and resource utilization and load balancing (Mobile EC).

4.3   Security and Privacy Plane (SPP)

The vehicular architecture should evolve towards a software based architecture, using open source technologies, and designing a secured environment is essential. That is why the idea of "security by design" should be a basic principle of the future architecture. Trust, security, intrusion detection, privacy and anonymity preserving systems taking into account the features of the vehicular environment (distribution, mobility, topology, etc.) should be developed. Different tools, such as AI and Blockchain, could be used to improve security. However, the existing papers are in the proposal stage and many issues still have to be resolved [14].

4.4   Knowledge Plane (KP)

The KP is a new concept in the vehicular architecture. Therefore, the Applications Programming Interfaces (APIs) between this plane and the other planes (SPP, MOP, CDP) and the services provided by the KP to the other planes must be defined. Similarly, a standardized data retrieval process should be designed. Thanks to this KP, data from the SPP, MOP and CDP could be correlated and new services and new applications may be imagined, implemented and evaluated. This could include mobility and context-aware services. Finally, solutions enabling the deployment of a distributed KP should be developed.

5   Conclusions

Looking forward, the vehicular networks should be integrated into a global 5G system. However, the integration of the current C-ITS architecture in this system is not yet possible. Indeed, to make it possible, we have identified five key points that should be considered: network intelligence and automation, edge data processing, network control, environment virtualization, security and privacy.

Different papers have already presented solutions improving the C-ITS architecture. However, none of them have proposed an architecture meeting the five identified requirements. Therefore, in this paper, these different approaches are described and compared and a new vehicular architecture is proposed.

This architecture, unlike the previous works, is composed of four planes. Indeed, a Knowledge Plane, using AI and improving the other planes, is designed. Moreover, the integration of the Blockchain technology, within the Security and Privacy plane, is proposed to overcome the current challenges. This paper provides an overview of this architecture but also presents the benefits and the role of the different modules added to the C-ITS reference architecture. Finally, some of the main challenges of the deployment of this architecture are discussed.

References

1. Borcoci, E., Obreja, S., Vochin, M.: Internet of vehicles functional architectures-comparative critical study. In: The Ninth International Conference on Advances in Future Internet, AFIN (2017)
2. Campolo, C., Molinaro, A., Iera, A., Menichella, F.: 5G network slicing for vehicle-to-everything services. IEEE Wirel. Commun. **24**(6), 38–45 (2017)
3. Contreras, J., Zeadally, S., Guerrero-Ibanez, J.A.: Internet of vehicles: architecture, protocols, and security. IEEE Internet Things J. **5**(5), 3701–3709 (2017)
4. Contreras-Castillo, J., Zeadally, S., Guerrero Ibáñez, J.A.: A seven-layered model architecture for internet of vehicles. J. Inf. Telecommun. **1**(1), 4–22 (2017)
5. Dolui, K., Datta, S.K.: Comparison of edge computing implementations: fog computing, cloudlet and mobile edge computing. In: 2017 Global Internet of Things Summit (GIoTS), pp. 1–6. IEEE (2017)
6. ETSI EN 302 665 V1.1.1: Intelligent transport systems (ITS), communications architecture. European Standard (Telecommunications Series) (2010)
7. Gonzalez, A.J., Nencioni, G., Kamisiński, A., Helvik, B.E., Heegaard, P.E.: Dependability of the NFV orchestrator: state of the art and research challenges. IEEE Commun. Surv. Tutor. **20**(4), 3307–3329 (2018)
8. 5G PPP Architecture Working Group: View on 5G architecture. White Paper, July 2016
9. Jiacheng, C., Haibo, Z., Ning, Z., Peng, Y., Lin, G., Xuemin, S.: Software defined internet of vehicles: architecture, challenges and solutions. J. Commun. Inf. Netw. **1**(1), 14–26 (2016)
10. Kaiwartya, O., Abdullah, A.H., Cao, Y., Altameem, A., Prasad, M., Lin, C.T., Liu, X.: Internet of vehicles: motivation, layered architecture, network model, challenges, and future aspects. IEEE Access **4**, 5356–5373 (2016)
11. Khan, H., Luoto, P., Bennis, M., Latva-aho, M.: On the application of network slicing for 5G-V2X. In: 24th European Wireless Conference on European Wireless 2018, pp. 1–6. VDE (2018)
12. Macedo, D.F., dos Santos, A.L., Nogueira, J.M.S., Pujolle, G.: A knowledge plane for autonomic context-aware wireless mobile ad hoc networks. In: Pavlou, G., Ahmed, T., Dagiuklas, T. (eds.) MMNS 2008. LNCS, vol. 5274, pp. 1–13. Springer, Heidelberg (2008). https://doi.org/10.1007/978-3-540-87359-4_1

13. Mendiboure, L., Chalouf, M.A., Krief, F.: Towards a blockchain-based SD-IoV for applications authentication and trust management. In: Skulimowski, A.M.J., Sheng, Z., Khemiri-Kallel, S., Cérin, C., Hsu, C.-H. (eds.) IOV 2018. LNCS, vol. 11253, pp. 265–277. Springer, Cham (2018). https://doi.org/10.1007/978-3-030-05081-8_19

14. Zheng, Z., Xie, S., Dai, H.N., Chen, X., Wang, H.: Blockchain challenges and opportunities: a survey. Int. J. Web Grid Serv. **14**(4), 352–375 (2018)

Impact of Driver Reaction and Penetration Rate on GLOSA

Mouna Karoui, Antonio Freitas, and Gerard Chalhoub[✉]

LIMOS-CNRS - University Clermont Auvergne, Clermont-Ferrand, France
{mouna.karoui,antonio.freitas,gerard.chalhoub}@uca.fr

Abstract. Cooperative Intelligent Transport Systems (C-ITS) aim to provide innovative solutions that can contribute to a better road management. Green Light Optimal Speed Advisory (GLOSA) is one of the traffic efficiency ITS services that can enhance traffic fluidity and fuel consumption economy. In this paper, we present driver reaction impact on GLOSA performance through a realistic simulation scenario taking into account the variation of penetration rate. In our work, we use vehicular network architecture ITS-G5 and we test our simple segment approach algorithm under a realistic traffic topology. Results show that driver reaction can significantly influence GLOSA performance in terms of fuel consumption and number of stopped vehicles.

Keywords: C-ITS · GLOSA · ITS-G5/IEEE802.11p

1 Introduction and Related Work

The high level of CO_2 emission seems to be a serious problem that threatens human being and environment. This issue is highly related to the cars fuel consumption and traffic jams. C-ITS systems offer solutions for traffic efficiency and road security. Various research institutes and industrial firms are interested in developing safety applications and traffic management services, helping the driver to avoid road hazards as well as optimizing the driving experience to be more comfortable and eco-friendly. Among the existing solutions, Green Light Optimal Speed Advisory (GLOSA) is one of the efficiency and management ITS services that give speed advice to the driver in order to cross traffic light at green phase. It could avoid stop and go phenomena behind the traffic light, thus it contributes to the reduction of fuel consumption. Two approaches of GLOSA are introduced in literature:

- **Single segment approach** that gives speed advice to pass traffic light taking into consideration the next corresponding intersection.
- **Multi-segment approach** which gives a speed advice taking into account not only the upcoming traffic light, but considering a set of the next intersections.

© Springer Nature Switzerland AG 2019
B. Hilt et al. (Eds.): Nets4Cars/Nets4Trains/Nets4Aircraft 2019, LNCS 11461, pp. 16–26, 2019.
https://doi.org/10.1007/978-3-030-25529-9_2

In previous work, many authors studied and proposed different algorithms for GLOSA. In paper [1], authors evaluated GLOSA potentials in terms of average stop time and fuel consumption. The authors presented different driving strategies like using constant velocity, acceleration and deceleration. They measured waiting time, CO2 emissions and number of stops against penetration rate. Their proposed algorithms saved an average of fuel consumption of about 13.7%. Concerning the waiting time, their GLOSA algorithm achieved a gain of about 15%. In terms of total travel time, they didn't obtain significant improvements.

Paper [2] proposed a set of acceleration advice algorithms where they compared their results in different situations. The authors proposed acceleration advice minimizing speed changes algorithm. Their results showed an improvement of fuel consumption of 25 % for a traffic flow of 200 veh/h. They measured average delay for GLOSA and without GLOSA using simple traffic models and an Intelligent Driver Model (IDM). They also compared results when advice is given only to the leader vehicle and when it is given to the leader and follower vehicles. Using a simple traffic model, results showed an enhancement between 31 % and 32 % of average delay. Their algorithm enables to save an average of fuel consumption between 21% and 23%. Using IDM model, their acceleration advice algorithm gave an improvement of 48% of average delay and it saved 17% of fuel consumption.

Paper [3] proposed a novel optimal speed advisory strategy for continuous intersections. The authors applied their algorithm in the context of electric cars which are mainly characterized by low fuel consumption and low emissions. In this paper, the authors measured average fuel consumption, average passing time and total number of steps. With Their proposed solution, they realized a gain of about 46 % in terms of total number of stops. In terms of average fuel consumption, they showed that their algorithms enable to save about 30 %.

In paper [4], authors proposed a new algorithm for GLOSA. They studied the impact of traffic flow on the proposed approach. The authors compared the increasing ratio of travel time, fuel consumption and CO2 emission for equipped and non equipped vehicles. The proposed GLOSA approach performs well for a traffic demand less than 400 to 500 veh/h. In other situations, the efficiency levels of their algorithm were worse than scenarios without the GLOSA system.

We observe that all cited studies didn't studied the impact of driver reaction time on GLOSA. In our paper, we focus our interest on studying the impact of driver reaction on GLOSA simple segment approach. We present a realistic simulation scenario and we study the impact of the variation of penetration rate on global performance of GLOSA.

This paper is organized as follows. In Sect. 2, we present the idea of our algorithm. Section 3 proposes a performance evaluation for GLOSA in terms of speed, average stop time gain and fuel consumption gain. Finally, we conclude and we give some perspectives of our work in Sect. 4.

2   GLOSA Proposed Algorithm

In paper [5], we proposed a simple segment approach algorithm called SABIN
(Speed Advisory Boundary fINder) that offers the possibility either to pass as
fast as possible (at t1+δt) or as slow as possible (approximately at t2). The idea
is to calculate advisory speed boundaries for GLOSA application. According to
a certain strategy, we can choose an advisory speed between two boundaries $v1$
and $v2$.

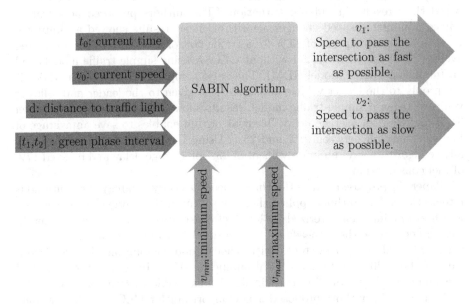

Fig. 1. Block diagram of SABIN algorithm (Color figure online)

As shown in Fig. 1, SABIN algorithm has the following input parameters:

- t_1 and t_2 are respectively the start and the end of the green phase.
- distance to traffic light d
- current time t_0
- Initial speed v_0

At the beginning, it calculates arrival time using maximum authorized speed and
compares its value with the end of the green phase time $t2$. This test enables
us to define cases in which driver can't pass on the current green phase. So, we
need to repeat the algorithm in order to get an adequate advisory speed for the
upcoming green phase. In the next section, we use the same algorithm to study
the driver reaction impact on GLOSA. Then, we produce results using realistic
traffic conditions.

3 Performance Evaluation

In this section, we present the simulation framework and its capabilities. We also describe the different settings of the simulation scenario. Then, we present results in terms of fuel consumption and average stop time gain varying the penetration rate which is defined as the level of vehicles equipment. The penetration rate variation is modeled according to a uniform probability distribution where vehicles are randomly equipped.

3.1 Simulation Environment

In our study, we chose Artery[1] as a simulation framework. Artery uses OMNeT++ as a network simulation platform and SUMO as a traffic mobility simulator. Figure 2 illustrates the simulation architecture that offers the possibility to produce a coupled simulation between network and traffic simulator. Thus, network simulator can get traffic information like speed and fuel consumption from traffic simulator using Traffic Control Interface (TraCI).

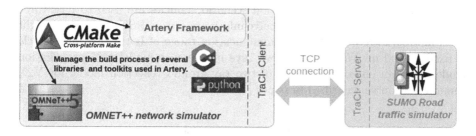

Fig. 2. Simulation architecture

In addition, this simulation architecture is characterized by its flexibility to simulate intelligent transport systems in a realistic environment [6]. This is one of the reasons that justify our simulation tool choice. In fact, SUMO is a microscopic traffic simulator that uses car-following models. These models describe how the following vehicle reacts with the leader vehicle in the same lane. It also proposes a formulation for this interaction taking into account many parameters such as gap between vehicles, length of vehicles and positions. Using this traffic simulation model, we are able to study the driver reaction on GLOSA speed advice acceptance.

3.2 Simulation Scenario

In this section, we describe the simulation scenario which consists of an urban road section of Bordeaux city[2] as shown in Fig. 3.

---

[1] https://github.com/riebl/artery.
[2] https://www.openstreetmap.org/#map=17/44.86316/-0.65115.

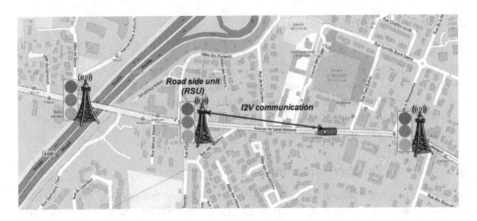

Fig. 3. Traffic topology imported from Open Street Map

The road topology is composed of a set of traffic lights. We set 3 RSUs, for each traffic light one RSU. Assuming that the position of the RSU and traffic light are the same. In this simulation scenario, vehicles are used to pass three successive traffic lights. Vehicles receive information from RSU about traffic light state and distance every 0.5 s. Communication range of both RSU and vehicle is fixed to 900 m. We also used two rays interference model as a propagation model. It is an enhanced version of two ray ground reflection model for V2X communication as described in paper [7].

Table 1. Mobility traffic simulation parameters

Car following model settings	
Car following model	Krauss
Minimum gap between vehicles	0.5 m
Driver time headway τ	0.1 s
Action length step of vehicle	0.1 s–2 s
Step length of simulation	0.1 s
Vehicle settings	
Vehicle category	Passenger
Vehicle length	5 m
Max speed	50 km/h
Min speed	20 km/h
Acceleration	1 m/s^2
Deceleration	2 m/s^2
Emission model	PHEMlight Gasoline Euro 4

We also suppose that each traffic light changes its phases at the same time with a periodic cycle of 60 s composed of the three following states: red (30 s), green (25 s) and amber (5 s). Table 1 summarizes road traffic configuration, such as car following model, the maximum authorized speed, maximum acceleration as well as the consumption model of the vehicle.

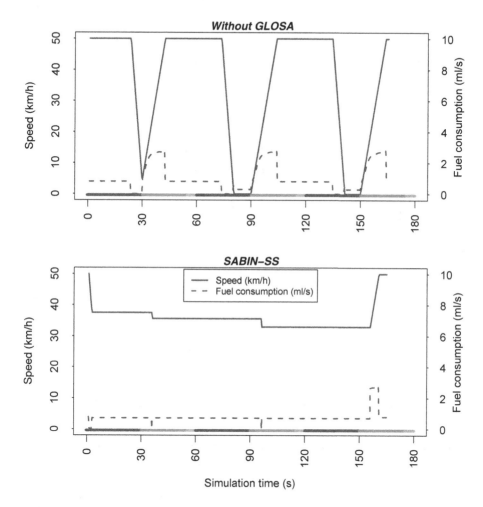

Fig. 4. Instantaneous speed and fuel consumption comparison between GLOSA and without GLOSA

Figure 4 presents speed and fuel consumption comparison between non equipped vehicle and a vehicle with GLOSA. Equipped vehicle adapts its speed according to traffic light changes. It decelerates to pass the traffic light at green. So, it enables driver to avoid stop and go phenomena. Thus, it reduces fuel consumption as shown in Fig. 4.

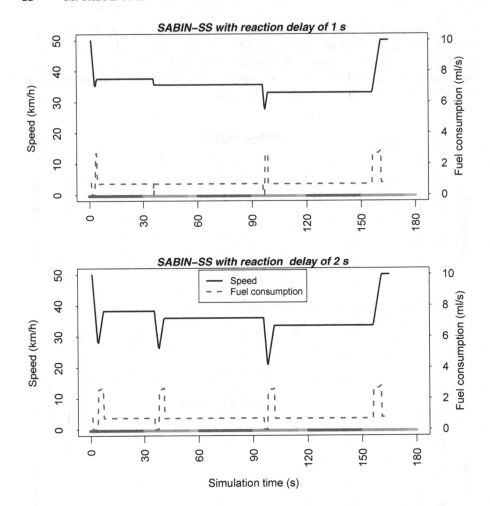

Fig. 5. Impact of reaction delay on speed for one equipped vehicle

Figure 5 illustrates speed of an equipped vehicle using a reaction delay of 1 and 2 s. For this case, we observe that speed advice is always taken with a delay. This reaction time significantly influences fuel consumption.

As shown in Table 2, for autonomous driving use case, single equipped vehicle achieves a fuel consumption gain of 24%. For human driving reaction time between 1 and 2 s, the fuel consumption gain scales between 23% and 15%.

Figure 6 shows the variation of average stop time gain against penetration rate variation. Average stop time gain is calculated as follows:

$$StopTimeGain(\%) = \frac{(X - Y)}{X} * 100$$

where X and Y are respectively the average stop time of Non equipped vehicles and equipped vehicles. For this simulation scenario, traffic flow is fixed to 800

Table 2. Fuel consumption gain summary for single traveling vehicle

Reaction delay (s)		Fuel consumption gain (%)
Autonomous driving	0.1	24.42
Human driving	1	23
	1.5	21.37
	2	15.01

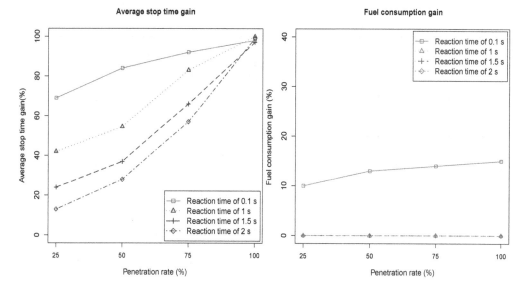

Fig. 6. Stop time gain   **Fig. 7.** Fuel consumption gain

veh/h which is equivalent to a traffic demand of 1 vehicle every 4.5 s and a total number of vehicles of 223. We observe that vehicles with autonomous driving achieve an average stop time gain between 70% and 97% varying the penetration rate from 25% to 100%. For vehicles with a static driver reaction delay of 2 s, the gain decreases to less than 20% for a penetration rate of 25%. This is explained by the accumulation of stop delay of leader vehicles that can be non equipped, thus it influences all the following vehicles.

Figure 7 presents the impact of penetration rate variation on fuel consumption gain. For reaction delay of 0.1 s, we achieve a fuel consumption gain between 10% and 15% for a penetration rate between 25% and 100%. For vehicles with reaction delay between 1 and 2 s, no fuel consumption gain is observed. This is due to the behavior of following vehicles which are highly affected by the reaction delay of the leader vehicle. Another factor influences total fuel consumption, which is the distance between vehicles, this distance changes according to the current speed and it is closely related to reaction distance. That's why, some collisions between vehicles occur when reaction time is higher than 0.1 s. Due to that, follower vehicles can be forced to stop or to decelerate. This is what explains that even with 100% of penetration rate, in case of human driver reactions, we didn't observe any fuel consumption enhancements.

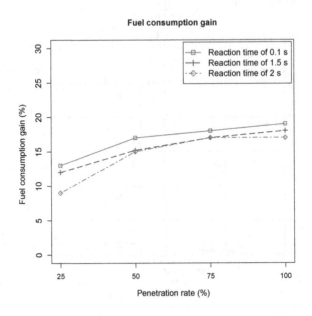

Fig. 8. Fuel consumption gain in case of a traffic flow of 400 veh/h

In Fig. 8, we evaluated fuel consumption under a free-collision scenario using a traffic flow of about 400 veh/h which is equivalent to a traffic demand of 1 vehicle every 9 s and a total vehicle number of about 112 vehicles. For this scenario, we considered safety distance between vehicles of about 30 m which is equivalent to 2 s of driver time headway. For this scenario, our findings show that fuel consumption gain, in case of autonomous driving, scales between 13% and 19% for a penetration rate between 25% and 100%. For Human driving reactions between 1.5 and 2 s, fuel consumption gain reaches respectively 12% and 9% for a penetration rate of 25%. And under a penetration rate of 100%, it reaches respectively 18% and 17%. We confirm that fuel consumption is not only influenced by reaction driver delays, but it also highly depends on traffic conditions. We also observed that it is important to consider an optimal safety distance between vehicles in order to avoid emergency braking cases, consequently, reduce fuel consumption.

4   Conclusion and Perspectives

In this work, we studied the impact of driver reaction and penetration rate on GLOSA. Our algorithm gives an average stop time gain between above 60% and

97% for immediate driver reaction. For driver reaction time between 1 and 2 s, we observe a deterioration of average stop time gain especially for a penetration rate between 25% and 75%. For a distribution where vehicles are totally equipped, stop time gain is less affected by driver reaction time.

For this scenario configuration, vehicles with immediate reaction achieved a fuel consumption gain between 10% to 15% respectively for a penetration rate from 25% to 100%. For vehicles with reaction delay between 1 and 2 s, no fuel consumption gain is observed. This is due to the impact of reaction time on the following vehicles, which causes collisions between vehicles due to non respected safety distance.

We also evaluated fuel consumption in collision-free scenario of 400 veh/h. We achieved a fuel consumption gain between 12% and 9% for human driving reaction delay respectively between 1.5 and 2 s. It also scales between respective values of 18% and 17% for a penetration rate of 100%. For this traffic flow conditions and autonomous driving case, we achieved a fuel consumption gain of 19%.

We conclude that driver reaction is an important criteria to take into account for GLOSA application. However, the main limitation of our study is that driver reaction time has a static variation, in which all drivers have a static behavior every time we change the action step length parameter in SUMO traffic simulator. In real-life, driver reaction changes from a person to another, it mainly depends on criteria such as age and emotional state.

In our future work, we will continue to investigate GLOSA service potentials and limitations focusing our interest on proposing a multiple segments approach algorithm and studying it in different traffic conditions.

Acknowledgement. This work is supported by C-ROADS France European project.

References

1. Eckhoff, D., Halmos, B., German, R.: Potentials and limitations of green light optimal speed advisory systems. In: 2013 IEEE Vehicular Networking Conference (VNC), pp. 103–110. IEEE (2013)
2. Stebbins, S., Hickman, M., Kim, J., Vu, H.L.: Characterising green light optimal speed advisory trajectories for platoon-based optimisation. Transp. Res. Part C Emerg. Technol. **82**, 43–62 (2017)
3. Luo, Y., Li, S., Zhang, S., Qin, Z., Li, K.: Green light optimal speed advisory for hybrid electric vehicles. Mech. Syst. Signal Process. **87**, 30–44 (2017)
4. Suzuki, H., Marumo, Y.: A new approach to green light optimal speed advisory (GLOSA) systems and its limitations in traffic flows. In: Ahram, T., Karwowski, W., Taiar, R. (eds.) IHSED 2018. AISC, vol. 876, pp. 776–782. Springer, Cham (2019). https://doi.org/10.1007/978-3-030-02053-8_118
5. Karoui, M., Freitas, A., Chalhoub, G.: Efficiency of speed advisory boundary finder (SABIN) strategy for GLOSA using ITS-G5. In: 2018 IFIP/IEEE International Conference on Performance Evaluation and Modeling in Wired and Wireless Networks (PEMWN), pp. 1–6. IEEE (2018)

6. Riebl, R., Günther, H.J., Facchi, C., Wolf, L.: Artery: extending veins for vanet applications. In: 2015 International Conference on Models and Technologies for Intelligent Transportation Systems (MT-ITS), pp. 450–456. IEEE (2015)
7. Sommer, C., Joerer, S., Dressler, F.: On the applicability of two-ray path loss models for vehicular network simulation. In: 2012 IEEE Vehicular Networking Conference (VNC), pp. 64–69. IEEE (2012)

Unsupervised Driving Profile Detection Using Cooperative Vehicles' Data

Brice Leblanc, Emilien Bourdy, Hacène Fouchal, Cyril de Runz$^{(\boxtimes)}$, and Secil Ercan

CReSTIC (*MODECO), Université de Reims Champagne-Ardenne, Reims, France
{brice.leblanc,emilien.bourdy,hacene.fouchal,
cyril.de-runz,secil.ercan}@univ-reims.fr

Abstract. C-ITS (Cooperative Intelligent Transport Systems) provide nowadays a very huge amounts of data either from vehicles, roadside units, operator servers or smart-phone applications. Data need to be exploited and analyzed. In this paper, we first study the communication logs containing network messages emitted by the vehicles and the infrastructures when they communicate. We used these logs to measure the latency and evaluate if it is consistent with data analysis. Then, we try to detect driving profile using unsupervised machine learning approaches. Results both in terms of latency and of driving profile detection reveal promising issues in this new area.

1 Introduction

The deployment of connected vehicles is an interesting challenge since a decade. Indeed, a dedicated WIFI has been designed for connected vehicles [1]: IEEE 802.11p[1] (denoted also ETSI ITS-G5 [2]). Therefore, the vehicles generate a lot of data when they have to respect the usual protocols defined by the ETSI, ISO and other standard institutes. In the meantime, many interested actors (road operators, telecom operators, car manufacturers) want and need to explore these data for many purposes as traffic prediction, driver profile detection, alternative route search, *etc.*

In order to do it, several principles over communication have to be evaluated and verified. In this paper, we present a case study where several vehicles were communicating together and with road side communication devices. A first study presented in this paper is about the communication latency. Indeed, latency is a key question when communications should inform about road traffic and road state in order to minimize risks. Moreover, latency is also a key information in order to detect driving profile through logs where cars are trying to preserve privacy [3]. The protection of privacy is an important challenge for ITS among many others [4] and big data approach can be a threat to it [5].

Supported by The InterCor project number INEA/CEF/TRAN/M2015/1143833.
[1] https://www.standards.its.dot.gov/Factsheets/Factsheet/80.

B. Hilt et al. (Eds.): Nets4Cars/Nets4Trains/Nets4Aircraft 2019, LNCS 11461, pp. 27–37, 2019.
https://doi.org/10.1007/978-3-030-25529-9_3

The main idea in this paper is to use unsupervised data mining approach in order to check if we are able to extract driver profiles on real data collected during a road driving Test. In this paper a driving profil is defined as a driving behavior identified regarding specific paterns. In order to do it, several scalable approaches from the literature were tested.

The paper is structured as follows. Section 2 is devoted to a state-of-the-art of unsupervised data mining approaches. Section 3 introduces the Test scenarios that provide driving data. Section 4 presents the results of the different unsupervised approaches over our real data. Section 5 gives the conclusion and perspectives.

2   Clustering: State of the Art

As previously indicated, the main purpose of this work is to try to detect driving profile through vehicles' communication data without information over the vehicles.

In machine learning there are different approaches to handle the data and extract information from it. According to our goal, this paper focus on the clustering techniques.

Clustering is a set supervised or unsupervised techniques that group data according to similarities based on a specified distance and other options without apriori. Without a high knowledge database clustering algorithms can find patterns in data. There is a wide variety of clustering algorithms that can be applied on many types of data. Many of classic algorithms have optimized variation for specific (or not) types of data and many scalable versions exist too.

The major fields of research and popular algorithm are presented in the following.

– Hierarchical-based algorithms

  A hierarchical clustering algorithm (HCA) [6] is a technique about clustering based on successive agglomerations or divisions of clusters. For agglomerative approaches as **Agnes**(**Ag**glomerative **Nes**ting), in the beginning, each data point is a cluster. At each step, the two closest clusters are merged together until all points are in the same cluster. To obtain the final clusters, the agglomeration tree is cut when the number of clusters meets the number of classes. For divisive approach as **Diana** (**Di**visive **An**alysis), the initialization is a cluster containing all data points. For each step, the most dissimilar data point is separated from the main cluster, form a new cluster and all data points that are more similar to it are gathered in it. There is different methods to select how the data to agglomerate or to divide, they are labelled as *linkage*

  BIRCH (Balanced Iterative Reducing and Clustering using Hierarchies) [7] is used to find clusters in large data-sets using small size memory and time. It uses the concept of Clustering Feature (CF) that is a kind of a summary of a cluster and a CF-Tree. Its strength is the ability to produce clusters with only one scan of the whole data-set. The result can be improved using additional small scans of the data-set. Readers are invited to refer to [8] for Birch variation and Spark compliant version.

– Partitionning-based algorithms

The **K-Means** [9] algorithm concept is to select at random k (k is a number defined by user) data points, to consider them as a cluster and to regroup the other points in the closest cluster until all points are inside a cluster. The center of the cluster is the mean of all the data points of the cluster and it is updated after a new point is added to the cluster. It is very simple and very efficient for many small data sets. Several versions of scalable k-means such as [10].

The **K-Medoïds** [11] algorithm works as K-Means algorithm but don't rely on an average of a cluster center but on the most representative data point of the cluster.

CURE (Clustering Using Representatives) [12] is more robust to outliers than K-Means and can identify non-spherical shape cluster but it is not scalable due to it's $\mathcal{O}$ (n^2 log n) time complexity.

– Density-based algorithms

The **DBSCAN** (Density-based Algorithm for discovering clusters in large spatial databases with noise) [13] is a fast algorithm with a strong resistance to outliers. It is widely use for it's effectiveness but it is very weak to cluster with varying density. This is the reason that led to the development of **OPTICS** (Ordering points to identify the clustering structure) [14]; it can handle the varying density of the cluster but at the cost of some speed performance.

– Grid-based algorithms

CLIQUE (Automatic Subspace Clustering of High Dimensional Data) [15] can automatically find the subspaces of the highest dimensionality, does not presume of any distribution because it is insensitive to the order of the data and it is linearly scalable. But like every grid-based algorithm the quality of the cluster depends of the number and width of partitions and grid cells parameters.

STING (Statistical Information Grid) [16] uses multiple layer of grid organized in a tree structure and statistical information of the cells is stored to answer to queries. It has the strength of having a very low computational complexity $\mathcal{O}(k)$ (where k is the number of grid cells at the lowest level), to be query-independent (the statistical information don't need queries to exist) and to be easily parallelized. It is also handling incremental updates (when the data is updated there is no need to recompute all the information in the cell hierarchy). However the biggest disadvantage is the loss of accuracy due to the probabilistic nature of the method.

– Artificial Neural Network algorithms

Unlike previous algorithm, algorithm using artificial neural networks can not handle a data-set immediately but needs to be trained beforehand. Once trained they can efficiently handle larger amounts of data than previous algorithm in a short time with a strong accuracy. **SOM** (Self Organized Map) [17] is an artificial neural network trained to produce a low-dimensional and discretized representation of the data. This makes it a strong visualization tool for high dimensional data. The **Neural Gas** [18] is inspired by SOM and that has multiple applications and one of them is the clustering [19]. It is an algorithm that can find in feature vectors an optimal representation of the data.

– Exemplar selection

   In [20], Bourdy *et al.* proposes a new approach of the classical k Nearest Neighbor (kNN) techniques to select exemplars, also called samples. Unlike the kNN techniques, this algorithm does not require a training set to select the exemplars. The data with the highest neighborhood density is the first selected sample, and then, we remove it and its neighborhood from the dataset. The next samples are selected in the same way.

We have described different scalable clustering techniques that can be applied to C-ITS communication data in order to extract driving profiles. We will present in the next section the application of some of these algorithms on real driving data. We will also present how C-ITS work.

3   Test Scenarios

3.1   Preliminaries

In the area of C-ITS (Cooperative Intelligent Transportation System), a protocol stack has been defined and standardized by the ETSI standardization institute in Europe[2]. Over the *Transport-Networking* layer (defined as geo-networking layer), the *Facilities* layer has been designed in order to be an efficient interface between the application layer (close to the driver and the vehicle sensors) and the *Transport-Networking* layer. Many types of messages are provided by this layer and we will focus in this study only on 2 main messages: CAM (Cooperative Awareness Message) [21] and DENM (Decentralized Environmental Notification Message) [22]. The aim behind sending CAM messages is to give dynamic information about the vehicle (i.e. position, speed, heading, etc.). A vehicle sends CAMs to its neighborhood using Vehicle-to-Vehicle (V2V) or V2I communications. Depending on the speed of the vehicle, the frequency of CAM messages varies from 1 Hz to 10 Hz. A vehicle sends DENM messages to notify about any type of event (i.e. accident, traffic jam, etc.). The event could be triggered automatically thanks to the connection to the vehicle CAN BUS or manually for sensitive cases as animal on the road.

The general architecture is presented on Fig. 1. Each station is supposed to have a set of pseudonym certificates.

A vehicle is able to send a message through a G5 network in order to reach its neighbours. The message could reach other vehicles thanks to multi-hop forwarding.

A Road Side Unit (RSU) plays the same role than a vehicle for the forwarding aspect. In addition to that, the RSU handle all received messages from

---

[2] ETSI: http://www.etsi.org.

Fig. 1. A general scheme for vehicle to vehicle communication

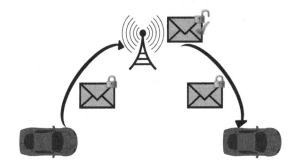

Fig. 2. A general scheme for vehicle to infrastructure communication

vehicles in order to run road operator's computations as traffic management, event recording. In some cases the RSU disseminates events towards other RSUs within operator's network. The ETSI has defined an ITS stack where the forwarding mechanism is achieved with the geo-networking protocol [23]. This layer plays the role of the networking layer.

The general vehicle to infrastructure communication scheme is illustrated on Fig. 2.

3.2   Test Scenarios

During the InterCor TestFest, four days of testing in real conditions on 30 km of urban road, 687 Mo of data have been collected (Tlog and pcap) produced by 16 vehicle and 4 Road Side Unit. For each RSU an average of 10Ko of Tlog is collected for each day so almost the total of the data collected is in pcap format. Moreover, 9 tablets where provided to 9 vehicles, to get their positions for the different tracks.

3.3   Network Communication Evaluation

The TestFest 2018 produced a large range of data, for instance 133249 CAM messages have been received by the roadside unit from vehicles. According to it, and in order to view if those data are compliant with traffic data analysis and driving profile identification, it is important to evaluate the communication latency. If the latency is globally too high, there is an issue both for the data analysis but much more for the pertinence of the deployed network.

Therefore, the latency have been calculated between vehicle (OBU) and roads operators (RSU) and are presented in Figs. 3, 4 and Table 1.

We have four On Board Unit separated in group of two to ease the comparison. The OBUs sends messages and the RSUs receive and decode it. The delay between sending and the end of the treatment is our latency. It is displayed according to the density of the neighborhood. We can see that, in the first graph, even with a dense neighborhood the latency does not exceed 500 ms.

In the second graph, OBU4 reaches more than 10 s of latency. It is due to time format problems during the registration of the log we use. This particular vehicle's time is not synchronize with the others.

The Table 1 shows statistics for all the combination of different types of stations for each days. We can see that the overall latency is quite low but sometimes some messages have a very high latency in comparison. Having theses latency on important messages can be problematic but for now we can suppose these result are due to time synchronization problem.

These result display that, even with a security layer on every messages, the G5 latency is globally acceptable for road safety usage and therefore, logs can be used to detect driving profiles as proposed in the next section.

Nevertheless, some communication strategies made by certain vehicles may produce safety issues as they are not informing as frequently as others about their states due to temporal issues. The strategy of other cars (very frequent emission) may also produce issues in terms of network overweight if plenty of vehicles are in the same area.

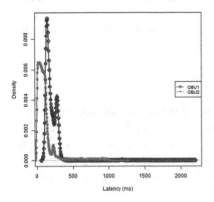

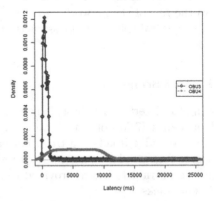

Fig. 3. Comparison of two OBU's latency of message send to an RSU

Fig. 4. Comparison of two other OBU's latency of message send to an RSU

The question of unsupervised driving profile extraction is important at least for privacy issues and is the core of the next section.

Table 1. Latency calculation between On Board Unit, Road Side Unit and Road Operators

	Day	Min	1^{st}Qu.	Median	Mean	3^{rd}Qu.	Max
OBU-RSU	1	1.0	94.0	188.0	236.9	350.0	930.0
OBU-RO	1	2.0	250.2	453.0	515.9	756.0	3106.0
RO-RSU	1	120.0	142.8	165.0	194.4	231.2	2152.0
OBU-RSU	2	36.0	2230.0	5068.0	5020.0	7896.0	10895.0
OBU-RO	2	1.0	44.0	92.0	137.5	147.0	1241.0
RO-RSU	2	18.7	100.3	268.6	364.3	582.0	1606.1
RO-RSU	3	1.0	40.0	78.0	121.7	120.0	1095.0
RO-RSU	4	1.0	38.0	79.0	128.2	120.5	1013.0

4 Data Analysis

From the data provided by the scenarios presented in the previous section we extracted the data generated by the vehicles equipped with tablets when they had to slow down or stop (red traffic light, stop sign, toll, etc.) displayed in Fig. 6. These extracted observations created our data set of 58 observations of 95 variables for the 9 different vehicles (for the other vehicles' trajectories the data were insufficient to extract enough observations).

In order to reveal/extract driving (sub)profiles, some of the clustering algorithms presented in the state of the art section were exploited. As indicated in Sect. 2, the selected approaches can generally be deployed using map/reduce paradigm and thus can be considered as scalable.

On the one hand, we have applied the classic partitionning algorithms (K-Means, K-Medoïds), the agglomerative algorithms (AGNES, DIANA), and a density based algorithm (DBSCAN) with normalized data and the results about the purity index are displayed in 2. The purity is an index that estimates the difference between the clustering expectation and the result of the algorithms. Here is the formula

$$PI = \frac{1}{n} \sum_{q=1}^{k} max_{i \leq j \leq l}(n_q^j)$$

where n is the total number of samples and k is the number of samples in the cluster q, that belong, to original class j ($1 \leq j \leq l$). The larger the value of purity is, the better the clustering performance is. The purer the clusters are, the better they represent one driving (sub)profile.

According to the previous figures, as obtained clusters are globally impure (they mixed data from different drivers), we can conclude that none of these classical algorithms produced convincing results as the obtained clusters do not represent real driving profiles or sub-profiles.

Table 2. Purity table

Algorithm	Purity
K-Means	0.379
K-Medoïds	0.345
AGNES	0.345
DIANA	0.328
CLARA	0.324
DBSCAN	0.224

On the other hand, the approach of Bourdy et al. [20] was applied. The results are presented in Table 3. According to them, when the density is less or equal to 24% ($k \leq 14$), the exemplars are grouping observations (trajectories) on their on driver, and with a density of 82% ($k = 48$), only 7 of the exemplars have neighbors from an other driver, i.e. 87,9% of observations are grouping with an exemplar from the same driver. The Fig. 5 graphically illustrate the latter. Exemplars are the big shapes and their neighborhood (grouping observations) are the small linked shapes for density. We can see that only seven of the samples are linked with data printed with a different shape and color.

Indeed, the produced exemplars may be view as driving profile representatives. Those results can reveal a privacy issue. Indeed, even though no driver information is used, by grouping data, according to Bourdy *Bourdy et al.* approach, we can identify a driving sub-profile. Nevertheless, the number of exemplars should moderate the conclusion.

Table 3. Different values of k with Intercor TestFest data

k	Density	Number of exemplars	Sampling distribution	Samples number representing other classes
7	12%	57	(6, 8, 5, 2, 4, 9, 7, 3, 13)	0
10	17%			
14	24%		(7, 7, 5, 2, 4, 9, 7, 3, 13)	
19	33%	53	(6, 7, 5, 2, 4, 9, 7, 2, 11)	4
29	50%	44	(6, 7, 4, 2, 3, 7, 5, 1, 9)	7
38	66%	40	(6, 5, 4, 2, 3, 6, 5, 1, 8)	
48	82%	34	(7, 4, 3, 0, 3, 5, 4, 2, 6)	

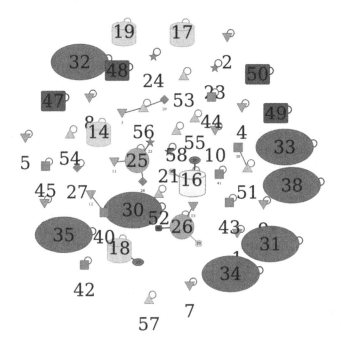

Fig. 5. Exemplar neighborhood with a k value of 48

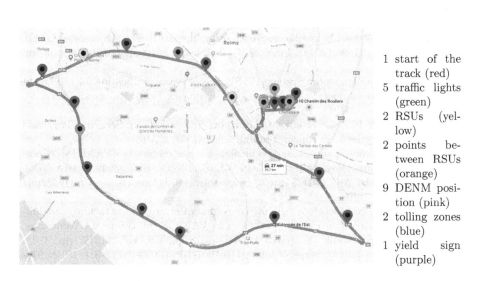

1 start of the track (red)
5 traffic lights (green)
2 RSUs (yellow)
2 points between RSUs (orange)
9 DENM position (pink)
2 tolling zones (blue)
1 yield sign (purple)

Fig. 6. TestFest track

5   Conclusion

In this paper, we have proposed a set of algorithms in order to analyze data provided by connected vehicles. We explained the results obtained from our experiments with 20 vehicles. The obtained delays are generally acceptable in the domain of C-ITS.

From this base, 58 trajectories from 9 vehicles were extracted. The aim of this paper is to try if clustering approaches may allow identifying interesting patterns in terms of driving profiles. According to our tests, the method presented by Bourdy *et al.* seems to give better results. This approach is scalable and portable using map/reduce.

As a future works, in term of data analysis, we will keep exploring the density approach with more algorithm and still take a look at grid and artificial neural network methods to see if they can provide good results too. We believe that combination of density approach with ANN and Grid or Graph can provide significant results. As vehicles' communication data can be view as streams from high dynamic networks, and due to the fact that C-ITS will produce soon enormous quantities of data, we will consider streaming clustering too. We plan to test better the scalability of our system by launching simulations. In the meantime we intend to analyze some other indicators related to the security, privacy and authenticity.

References

1. Teixeira, F.A., et al.: Vehicular networks using the IEEE 802.11P standard. Veh. Commun. **1**(2), 91–96 (2014). ISSN 2214-2096. https://doi.org/10.1016/j.vehcom.2014.04.001
2. ETSI. Intelligent Transport Systems (ITS); Access layer specification for Intelligent Transport Systems operating in the 5 GHz frequency band. European Standard. ETSI, November 2012
3. ETSI. ETSI TS 102 941: Intelligent Transport Systems (ITS); Security; Trust and Privacy Management. European Standard. ETSI, May 2018
4. Akalu, R.: Privacy, consent and vehicular ad hoc networks (VANETs). Comput. Law Secur. Rev. **34**(1), 37–46 (2018). ISSN 0267-3649. https://doi.org/10.1016/j.clsr.2017.06.006. http://www.sciencedirect.com/science/article/pii/S0267364917302170
5. Saini, I., Saad, S., Jaekel, A.: Identifying vulnerabilities and attacking capabilities against pseudonym changing schemes in VANET. In: Traore, I., Woungang, I., Ahmed, S.S., Malik, Y. (eds.) ISDDC 2018. LNCS, vol. 11317, pp. 1–15. Springer, Cham (2018). https://doi.org/10.1007/978-3-030-03712-3_1. ISBN 978-3-030-03712-3
6. Kaufman, L., Rousseeuw, P.J.: Finding Groups in Data: An Introduction to Cluster Analysis. Wiley, Hoboken (1990)
7. Zhang, T., Ramakrishnan, R., Livny, M.: BIRCH: an efficient data clustering method for very large databases. In: Proceedings of the 1996 ACM SIGMOD International Conference on Management of Data, SIGMOD 1996, Montreal, Quebec, Canada, pp. 103–114. ACM (1996). ISBN 0-89791-794-4. https://doi.org/10.1145/233269.233324

8. Lorbeer, B., et al.: Variations on the clustering algorithm BIRCH. Big Data Res. **11**, 44–53 (2018). Selected papers from the 2nd INNS Conference on Big Data: Big Data & Neural Networks, pp. 44–53. ISSN 2214–5796. https://doi.org/10.1016/j.bdr.2017.09.002. http://www.sciencedirect.com/science/article/pii/S2214579617300151

9. MacQueen, J.: Some methods for classification and analysis of multivariate observations. In: Proceedings of the Fifth Berkeley Symposium on Mathematical Statistics and Probability. Statistics, vol. 1, pp. 281–297. University of California Press, Berkeley (1967). https://projecteuclid.org/euclid.bsmsp/1200512992

10. Bahmani, B., et al.: Scalable K-means++. Proc. VLDB Endow. **5**(7), 622–633 (2012). ISSN 2150–8097. https://doi.org/10.14778/2180912.2180915

11. Kaufman, L., Rousseeuw, P.: Clustering by means of medoids. In: Statistical Data Analysis Based on the L1 Norm and Related Methods. North-Holland; Amsterdam, pp. 405–416 (1987). ISBN: 0444702733

12. Guha, S., Rastogi, R., Shim, K.: Cure: an efficient clustering algorithm for large databases. Inf. Syst. **26**(1), 35–58 (2001). ISSN 0306–4379. https://doi.org/10.1016/S0306-4379(01)00008-4

13. Ester, M., et al.: A density-based algorithm for discovering clusters in large spatial databases with noise. In: KDD, vol. 96, no. 34, pp. 226–231 (1996)

14. Ankerst, M., et al.: OPTICS: ordering points to identify the clustering structure. ACM Sigmod Rec. **28**(2), 49–60 (1999)

15. Agrawal, R., et al.: Automatic subspace clustering of high dimensional data for data mining applications, vol. 27, no. 2. ACM (1998)

16. Wang, W., Yang, J., Muntz, R., et al.: STING: a statistical information grid approach to spatial data mining. In: VLDB, vol. 97, pp. 186–195 (1997)

17. Kohonen, T.: Self-organized formation of topologically correct feature maps. Biol. Cybern. **43**(1), 59–69 (1982). ISSN 1432–0770. https://doi.org/10.1007/BF00337288

18. Martinetz, T., Schulten, K., et al.: A "neural-gas" network learns topologies (1991)

19. Canales, F., Chacón, M.: Modification of the growing neural gas algorithm for cluster analysis. In: Rueda, L., Mery, D., Kittler, J. (eds.) CIARP 2007. LNCS, vol. 4756, pp. 684–693. Springer, Heidelberg (2007). https://doi.org/10.1007/978-3-540-76725-1_71

20. Bourdy, E., Piamrat, K., Herbin, M., Fouchal, H.: New method for selecting exemplars application to roadway experimentation. In: Hodoň, M., Eichler, G., Erfurth, C., Fahrnberger, G. (eds.) I4CS 2018. CCIS, vol. 863, pp. 75–84. Springer, Cham (2018). https://doi.org/10.1007/978-3-319-93408-2_6

21. ETSI EN 302 637-2; Intelligent Transport Systems (ITS); Vehicular Communications; Basic Set of Applications; Part 2: Specification of Cooperative Awareness Basic Service. European Standard. ETSI, November 2014

22. ETSI EN 302 637-3; Intelligent Transport Systems (ITS); Vehicular Communications; Basic Set of Application; Part 3: Specifications of Decentralized Environmental Notification Basic Service. European Standard. ETSI, November 2014

23. ETSI EN 302 636-4-1; Intelligent Transport Systems (ITS); Vehicular Communications; GeoNetworking; Part 4: Geographical Addressing and forwarding for point-to-point and point-to-multipoint communications; Subpart 1: Media-Independent Functionality. European Standard. ETSI, July 2014

Cyber Attack Detection Algorithm Using Traffic Flow Theory

Marwane Ayaida[1]($\boxtimes$), Nadhir Messai[1], Sameh Najeh[2], and Geoffrey Wilhelm[1]

[1] CReSTIC, University of Reims Champagne-Ardenne, Reims, France
{marwane.ayaida,nadhir.messai,geoffrey.wilhelm}@univ-reims.fr
[2] Higher School of Communications of Tunis, COSIM Research Laboratory,
University of Carthage, Tunis, Tunisia
sameh.najeh@supcom.tn

Abstract. Vehicular ad hoc networks (VANETs) are expected to play an important role in our lives. They will improve the traffic safety and bring about a revolution on the driving experience. However, these benefits are counterbalanced by possible attacks that threaten not only the vehicle's security, but also passengers' lives. One of the most common attacks is the Sybil attack, which is even more dangerous than others because it could be the starting point of many other attacks in VANETs. This paper proposes a distributed approach allowing the detection of Sybil attacks by using the traffic flow theory. The key idea here is that each vehicle will monitor its neighborhood in order to detect an eventual Sybil attack. This is achieved by a comparison between the real accurate speed of the vehicle and the one estimated using the V2V communications with vehicles in the vicinity. This estimated speed is obtained using the traffic flow fundamental diagram of the road's portion where the vehicles are moving.

A mathematical model that evaluates the rate of Sybil attack detection according to the traffic density is proposed. Then, this model is validated through some numerical simulations conducted using MATLAB tool.

Keywords: ITS · VANETs · Traffic model · Sybil attack · CAM · Ad Hoc Network

1 Introduction

The new mobility challenges of vehicles in Smart Cities need the enhancement of Intelligent Transportation Systems (ITS) that helps to reduce congestions, accidents, fuel consumption, etc. Thus, Vehicular Ad Hoc Networks (VANETs), which are a major component of ITS, has been a subject of some intensive research and experimental applications in these last two decades. In such networks, vehicles on the road will communicate with each other to exchange information about their directions, their speeds, their positions, the state of road,

© Springer Nature Switzerland AG 2019
B. Hilt et al. (Eds.): Nets4Cars/Nets4Trains/Nets4Aircraft 2019, LNCS 11461, pp. 38–49, 2019.
https://doi.org/10.1007/978-3-030-25529-9_4

etc. Currently, the automotive industry is working to equip new vehicles with Wireless Access Vehicular Environment (WAVE) devices [1]. WAVE protocols are based on the IEEE 802.11p standard and provide the basic radio standard for dedicated short-range communication (DSRC).

Since a successful attack could have dramatic consequences, security of Vehicular Ad Hoc Networks becomes an important issue. A well known attack is the Sybil attack. This attack is considered as one of the most dangerous and the basis of many other attacks [2]. In Sybil attack, malicious node may assume multiple identities. The least harmful objective of such attack is to create an illusion of traffic congestion in order to reroute other vehicles from the road that the attacker will take. At the other end, the attacker could push a specific vehicle to take a particular route in order to trap it or, even, guide it straight to a crash in an accident. Therefore, detecting such attack is very sensitive for several safety, privacy and security reasons.

This paper presents a new technique allowing the detection of Sybil attack in VANETs networks. This approach exploits some traffic flow theory phenomena in order to generate a residual corresponding to the difference between the measured speed of the vehicle and the speed that this vehicle estimated in a distributed way by using the information of its surrounding. A significant deviation of this residual from a predefined threshold is considered as an indicator of a potential attack. Once a vehicle detects an attack, it notifies its neighbours allowing the detection of this attack thanks to a collaboration between the honest vehicles.

This algorithm is easy to be implemented and does need neither a central node nor additional hardware. Its efficiency was proven thanks to a mathematical model and a realistic numerical simulations.

The reminder of this paper is as follow. Section 2 describes some related works about Sybil attacks detection. Section 3 details how our detection algorithm works. Section 4 presents a mathematical model that evaluates the detection rate of the proposed Sybil attack algorithm. Section 5 evaluates this algorithm using a realistic network numerical simulation. Finally, Sect. 6 concludes this paper and gives some perspectives to this work.

2   Related Works

Many mechanisms that aim to detect Sybil attacks have been proposed. Among them, we can cite those based on resource testing [3] (i.e. computing ability, storage ability, communication bandwidth, etc.). The idea here is that each vehicle broadcasts to all its neighbors a request that needs some physical resources to be computed. Thus, since attackers have to reply simultaneously for them and for the created fake nodes, they will not be able to reply in the given interval time and only honest vehicles will be trusted. However, this approach wastes a lot of computing resources and bandwidth for these tests. Moreover, attackers equipped with powerful computing devices can bypass these tests.

Another common used solutions for defending against Sybil attacks are based on Public Key Infrastructure (PKI). Since the vehicle can be authenticated with its unique public key and certificate managed by the Root Authority (RA), an attacker can be detected at any time. Traditional PKI-based certificates include only key information and do not include any unique physical information related to the vehicle. This makes such approach potentially vulnerable to impersonation attack because any stolen valid key pair and certificate can be used by another malicious vehicle to create fake nodes with valid certificates. In multi-factor authentication scheme [4], the certificate contains not only the public key information but also a set of physical attribute values about the vehicle (i.e. the radio frequency fingerprint, etc.) recorded by the Certificate Authority (CA). Nevertheless, establishing such Public Key Infrastructure for individual vehicles [5,6] takes a long time. The use of a long-term key pairs and certificates can also make the tracking and the collecting of vehicles behaviors easier. PKI-based approaches are complex and expensive to be implemented in terms of equipments that have to be deployed. For example, we have to deploy a Root Authority (RA), a Long-Term Certificate Authority (LTCA) and a Pseudonym Certificate Authority (PCA), knowing that the PCA has to be reached by the vehicles in order to download new Pseudonym Certificates (PCs). Therefore, vehicles have to access to the PCA through the Road Side Units (RSUs). The deployment of these RSUs is estimated to end by 2026 with a cost of $660M$ [7]. Another alternative is to take advantage from the existing cellular networks to download certificates. However, drivers have to pay this access. Moreover, vehicles will overload the cellular network if they use this media since it was not initially sized to manage this task. Moreover, even if a vehicle with a valid Long-Term Certificate (LTC) is corrupted, but not yet identified as it is, it can continue to download PCs as needed. Therefore, the PKI protection stills available for new vehicles but not really for already involved corrupted vehicles. Since all the nodes are perceived as honest by each others, this makes the detection of Sybil attacks very difficult and subsequently more difficult the defense against them [8].

To tackle some limitations of the overviewed approach, this paper proposed to design an original Sybil attacks detection mechanism, which takes benefit from the traffic flow models already provided to the vehicle in order to detect Sybil attacks. This mechanism is easy to be implemented and very powerful as demonstrated by its evaluation through a mathematical model and some realistic simulations.

3   Presentation of the Proposed Algorithm

First, we will present a high-level description of this algorithm presented. Then, each step of this algorithm will be detailed in the second one as a pseudo-code algorithm.

3.1   Algorithm High-Level Description

The vehicle waits for the reception of a CAM (Cooperative Awareness Message) to start updating the list of neighbours in order to add the source node as a neighbour if it does not already exist since met for the first time. Otherwise, it updates the timestamp of this node. This is done continuously as stated by the CAM standard.

In order not to surcharge the processing of the vehicle, the Sybil attack detection procedure is launched according to a predefined period (T_{det}). Once the timer expires, the vehicle collects all the processing needed data. First, it extracts from the list of neighbors those that still in its vicinity. To do so, it refreshes the list by removing the nodes that were not seen a given time. The duration used for this cleaning could be tuned depending on the scenario and the environment used (urban, highway, etc.). Secondly, the fundamental diagram is used to estimate the speed of the vehicle (V_{est}). Note here that the FD could be already integrated directly in the On-Board Unit (OBU) of the vehicle or it could be downloaded from a Road Side Unit (RSU) at the city's entry for example. Then, it measures the real speed V. After that, the detection of the Sybil attack is achieved by a comparison of these two speeds (i.e. $|V - V_{est}|$). If this difference is lower than a predefined threshold value V_{th}, no attack detected. Otherwise, an orchestrated Sybil attack is detected and the affected vehicle will notify its neighbors of this attack. Finally, if the vehicle receives at least a confirmation from another vehicle that has do the same analysis, it will launch some already prepared countermeasures, which are out of scope of this paper. Otherwise, it will ignore this attack detection and restart another processing when receiving another CAM message.

Algorithm 1. Updating Neighbors' List

1: **procedure** NEIGHBORSUPDATING(Packet P, List Neighbors)
2:     **if** ($P.Sender \in Neighbors$) **then**
3:         $Neighbors[Sender].Timestamp \leftarrow P.Timestamp$;
4:         $Neighbors[Sender].Location \leftarrow P.Location$;
5:     **else**
6:         $Neighbors.Add(Sender)$;
7:         $Neighbors[Sender].Timestamp \leftarrow P.Timestamp$;
8:         $Neighbors[Sender].Location \leftarrow P.Location$;
9:     **end if**
10: **end procedure**

3.2 Algorithm Detailed Description

To better understand the proposed algorithm, we present here its most features depicted in the following algorithms:

- Algorithm 1 details the procedure of the neighbors' list updating.
- Algorithm 2 presents the procedure of the neighbors' number computing.
- Algorithm 3 shows the procedure that uses the traffic model to estimate the speed of the vehicle.

– Algorithm 4 describes the whole algorithm that uses the three previous algorithms.

Algorithm 2. Computing Number of Neighbors

1: **procedure** NUMBERNEIGHBORS(List Neighbors)
2:     int T_{th} : freshness of neighbors
3:     int N : number of neighbors
4:     **foreach** $(n \in Neighbors)$ **do**
5:         **if** $([Now - Neighbors[n].Timestamp] > T_{th})$ **then**
6:             $Neighbors.Remove(n)$;
7:         **end if**
8:     **end for**
9:     $N = Neighbors.size()$;
10:     *return N*;
11: **end procedure**

In the Algorithm 1, when a vehicle receives a CAM message, it verifies if it exists already in the neighbors' list. If it is the case, it has to update the location and the timestamp of the received message. Otherwise, it adds the new sender of the message as a neighbor and it inserts its location and its timestamp.

Algorithm 3. Estimating Speed

1: **procedure** SPEEDESTIMATION(List Neighbors)
2:     double V_{est} : estimated speed
3:     double a : constant of fluid area
4:     double b : constant of congested area
5:     double d_c : critical density
6:     double d_{max} : maximal density
7:     double $c = -b * d_{max}$: second constant of congested area
8:     double density : current density
9:     int Length : length of a segment
10:     density = (NumberNeighbors(Neighbors)+ 1) / Length;
11:     **if** $(density < d_c)$ **then**   ▷ Fluid Area
12:         $flow = a * density$;
13:     **else if** $(density < d_{max})$ **then**   ▷ Congested Area
14:         $flow = b * density + c$;
15:     **else**
16:         $flow = 0$;   ▷ Traffic Jam
17:     **end if**
18:     $Vest = flow/density$;
19:     *return V_{est}*;
20: **end procedure**

When a vehicle needs to compute the number of its neighbors, it starts by updating the list of its neighbors as detailed in the Algorithm 2. To do that, it verifies if the time since the receiving of the last message is higher than a given threshold (i.e. T_{th}). If so, it removes the neighbour from the list. The number of neighbours is then calculated as the cardinality of this updated list.

On the other hand, the vehicle's speed is estimated based on the macroscopic traffic model using the Fundamental Diagram (FD) as described by the Algorithm 3. To do this, we exploit the characteristics of the FD of the section in which the vehicle moves. This FD is supposed to be already stored in the vehicle within the map or downloaded from some specific RSUs.

The first step of the Algorithm 3 is to estimate the density, which depends on the length of the portion's road and the number of neighbors estimated according to the Algorithm 2. Note here that due to the constraints on the transmission range, each real road's portion is decomposed in some virtual segments with a length ($Length$) corresponding to the OBU's transmission range and characterized by the same FD. Once the density is estimated, the traffic flow is obtained using the FD characteristics according to the traffic's state (fluid, congested and jam). Finally, the speed is estimated using the traffic model.

Algorithm 4. Attack Detection

1: double V_{est} : estimated speed
2: double V : real speed
3: double V_{th} : threshold to detect a Sybil attack
4: List Neighbors : list of Neighbors
5: Time T_{det} : timer of periodic attack detection triggering
6: Time DetectionTime : timestamp of the attack detection
7: int Timeout : maximum waiting time for an attack confirmation
8: Packet CAM : packet CAM received
9: **while** ($ReceiveCAM(CAM)$) **do**
10:     $NeighborsUpdating(CAM, Neighbors)$;
11: **end while**
12: **if** (T_{det} is expired) **then**
13:     $V_{est} = SpeedEstimation(Neighbors)$;
14:     $V = Node.Mobility.GetSpeed()$;
15:     **if** ($|V - V_{est}| > V_{th}$) **then**
16:         $DetectionTime = Now$;
17:         $BrodcastMessage("AttackDetected")$;;
18:         $Wait(Timeout)$;
19:         **if** ($ReceiveConfirmation()$) **then**
20:             $LaunchCountermeasures(Sybil)$;
21:         **end if**
22:     **end if**
23:     T_{det} is armed
24: **end if**

If this difference is higher than the threshold V_{th}, a Sybil attack is then detected. Therefore, the vehicle broadcasts a notification message to its neighbours. If no confirmation is received after a custom duration (i.e. *Detection-Time*), the detection is considered as a false positive warning and subsequently neglected. On the other hand, if at least one other vehicle makes the same conclusion, the attack is confirmed and the vehicle will launch some countermeasures, which are out of focus of this paper.

One of the most important advantages of this standalone algorithm is the fact that it is deployed within the vehicle without needing neither extra hardware than the OBU, nor extra messages than CAM messages. It is regularly executed to monitor the neighbours in order to detect any attack.

After this description of the proposed approach, the following sections is dedicated to the validation of our algorithm through a mathematical model and some realistic simulations.

4   Mathematical Model Analysis

4.1   Problem Formulation

We consider in this section N_0 vehicles that actually exist and N_1 attacking vehicles. We denote $N_1 = \alpha N_0$, where α is the percentage of attacking vehicles. Our aim in this section is to determine a closed form of the sybil attack probability, denoted as P_{sya}, which can be defined as

$$P_{sya} \triangleq \mathbb{P}(V - V_{est} \geq V_{th}) \tag{1}$$

In the rest of the section, the velocity of the vehicle is defined as

$$\begin{cases} V = v_{m1} + \Delta V_1 : \text{ if the traffic is fluid} \\ V = v_{m2} + \Delta V_2 : \text{ if the traffic is congested} \\ V = v_{m3} + \Delta V_3 : \text{ otherwise} \end{cases} \tag{2}$$

where, v_{mi}, $i \in \{1, 2, 3\}$, is the mean velocity according to the traffic state (fluid, congested and jam), and ΔV_i is a gaussian distribution with zero mean and standard deviation σ_i.

4.2   Sybil Attack Probability Estimation

Proposition 1. *Within the hypothesis of triangular FD, a closed form of the sybil attack probability P_{sya} is given by*

$$P_{sya} = \frac{1}{2}[p_1 erfc(\frac{a - v_{m1} + V_{th}}{\sqrt{2}\sigma_1})$$
$$+ p_2 erfc(\frac{V_{th} - v_{m2} + b}{\sqrt{2}\sigma_2} + \frac{cL}{(\alpha + 1)\sqrt{2}N_0\sigma_2}) \tag{3}$$
$$+ p_3 erfc(\frac{V_{th} - v_{m3}}{\sqrt{2}\sigma_3})]$$

where, erfc is the Complementary Error Function, defined as

$$erfc(x) \triangleq \frac{2}{\sqrt{\pi}} \int_x^{+\infty} e^{-y^2} dy \qquad (4)$$

and where p_1, p_2 and p_3 are defined as follows

$$\begin{cases} p_1 = \mathbb{P}(\alpha < \frac{Ld_c}{N_0} - 1) \\ p_2 = \mathbb{P}(\frac{Ld_c}{N_0} - 1 \le \alpha < \frac{Ld_{max}}{N_0} - 1) \\ p_3 = \mathbb{P}(\alpha \ge \frac{Ld_{max}}{N_0} - 1) \end{cases} \qquad (5)$$

Proof. Based on the traffic model and by using the total probability theorem, we have

$$P_{sya} = \mathbb{P}(V \ge V_{est} + V_{th}, d < d_c)$$
$$+ \mathbb{P}(V \ge V_{est} + V_{th}, d_c \le d < d_{max}) \qquad (6)$$
$$+ \mathbb{P}(V \ge V_{est} + V_{th}, d_c \ge d_{max})$$

By applying the Bayes theorem, the first term of the previous equation can be expressed as

$$\mathbb{P}(V \ge V_{est} + V_{th}, d < d_c)$$
$$= \mathbb{P}(V \ge V_{est} + V_{th}|d < d_c)P(d < d_c) \qquad (7)$$

Then, one obtains easily for the fluid state

$$\mathbb{P}(V \ge V_{est} + V_{th}|d < d_c)$$
$$= \mathbb{P}(V \ge \frac{ad}{d} + V_{th}|d < d_c) \qquad (8)$$

In the same manner, we can show easily using (6) for the congested state gives

$$\mathbb{P}(V \ge V_{est} + V_{th}|d_c \le d < d_{max}$$
$$= \mathbb{P}(V \ge \frac{bd + c}{d} + V_{th}|d_c \le d < d_{max}) \qquad (9)$$

The 3rd term of Eq. (6), becomes by using the density $d \ge d_{max}$

$$\mathbb{P}(V \ge V_{est} + V_{th}|d \ge d_{max})$$
$$= \mathbb{P}(V \ge v_{th}|d \ge d_{max}) \qquad (10)$$

Then by considering that the density d is expressed as

$$d = \frac{N_0 + N_1}{L} \qquad (11)$$

Hence, by applying Eqs. (8), (9) and (11), the expression of P_{sya} becomes

$$P_{sya} = p_1 \mathbb{P}(V \ge a + V_{th})$$
$$+ p_2 \mathbb{P}(V \ge b + \frac{cL}{(1+\alpha)N_0} + V_{th}) + p_3 \mathbb{P}(V \ge V_{th}) \qquad (12)$$

The first term of the previous expression, can be expressed as

$$\mathbb{P}(V \geq a + V_{th}) = \mathbb{P}(\Delta V \geq v_0 + a - v_{m1})$$

$$= \int_{a - v_{m1} + V_{th}}^{+\infty} \frac{e^{\frac{-x^2}{2\sigma_1^2}}}{\sqrt{2\pi\sigma_1^2}} dx \tag{13}$$

Using the change of variable $y = \frac{x}{\sqrt{2}\sigma_1}$ and expression of the $erfc$ defined in Eq. (4), we have

$$\mathbb{P}(V \geq a + V_{th}) = \frac{1}{\sqrt{\pi}} \int_{\frac{V_{th} + a - v_{m1}}{\sqrt{2}\sigma_1}}^{+\infty} e^{-y^2} dy$$

$$= \frac{1}{2} erfc(\frac{V_{th} + a - v_{m1}}{\sqrt{2}\sigma_1}) \tag{14}$$

We proof in the same way that

$$\mathbb{P}(V \geq b + \frac{cL}{(\alpha + 1)N_0} + V_{th})$$

$$= \mathbb{P}(\Delta V \geq b + \frac{cL}{(\alpha + 1)N_0} + V_{th} - v_{m2})$$

$$= \int_{b + v_0 - v_{m2} + \frac{cL}{(\alpha+1)N_0}}^{+\infty} \frac{e^{\frac{-x^2}{2\sigma_2^2}}}{\sqrt{2\pi\sigma_2^2}} dx \tag{15}$$

Using the same change of variable as previously, we have trivially,

$$\mathbb{P}(V \geq b + \frac{cL}{(\alpha + 1)N_0} + V_{th})$$

$$= \frac{1}{\sqrt{\pi}} \int_{\frac{V_{th} - v_{m2} + b}{\sqrt{2}\sigma_2} + \frac{cL}{(\alpha+1)N_0\sqrt{2}\sigma_2}}^{+\infty} e^{-y^2} dy \tag{16}$$

from which it follows that

$$\mathbb{P}(V \geq b + \frac{cL}{(\alpha + 1)N_0} + V_{th})$$

$$= \frac{1}{2} erfc(\frac{V_{th} v_{m2} + b}{\sqrt{2}\sigma_2} + \frac{cL}{(\alpha + 1)\sqrt{2}N_0\sigma_2}) \tag{17}$$

By considering the Eq. (10), we obtain

$$\mathbb{P}(V \geq V_{est} + V_{th} | d \geq d_{max})$$

$$= \int_{V_{th} - v_{m3}}^{+\infty} \frac{e^{\frac{-x^2}{2\sigma_3^2}}}{\sqrt{2\pi\sigma_3^2}} dx \tag{18}$$

Using the same change of variable as previously, we have

$$\mathbb{P}(V \geq V_{th} - v_{m3}) = \frac{1}{\sqrt{\pi}} \int_{\frac{V_{th} - v_{m3}}{\sqrt{2}\sigma_3}}^{+\infty} e^{-y^2} dy$$
$$= \frac{1}{2} erfc(\frac{V_{th} - v_{m3}}{\sqrt{2}\sigma_3})$$

(19)

This completes the proof.

5 Simulations and Validation of the Proposed Algorithm

This section presents the environment and the results of the network simulation that we use to evaluate the efficiency of our proposed algorithm.

To test the effectiveness of our sybil attack detection mechanism, we have performed some simulations based on the mathematical formulation given in Proposition 1. These simulations are carried out using the parameter of the same FD that will be detailed in the simulation results (Sect. 5) as well as the parameters given in Table 1.

Table 1. Simulation parameters

Parameters	v_{m1}, v_{m2}, v_{m3}	ΔV_1^2, ΔV_2^2, ΔV_3^2
Values (m/s)	55, 13.8, 0.27	5.55, 2.77, 0.27

In Figs. 1 and 2, the P_{sya} is depicted versus N_0 ($10 \leq N_0 \leq 50$) and α ($0.5 \leq \alpha \leq 5$) respectively. In Fig. 1, we assume that we have 8 attackers (i.e. $\alpha = \frac{8}{N_0}$). This figure shows that more the number of the honest vehicle N_0 on the section is, higher the detection rate is. This can be explained by the fact that when the number of the vehicles is low, the traffic is fluid and the few chosen number of attackers does not have an effect on the speed estimation (the vehicles moves at the free speed). It is also interesting to note that if we increase the attacker number, the proposed algorithm can easily detect the Sybil attack as confirmed by Fig. 2. In fact, a Sybil attack is generally launched when the traffic is fluid in order to simulate a fake congestion and consequently it needs a high number of attackers. Figure 2 shows clearly that the more the number of attackers (α increasing), the higher the probability of detection even when the traffic is fluid. It shows also that the probability detection is higher when the number of honest nodes increases with the same number of attackers. This could be explained by the fact that the detection is easier in the congested area. Then, when the number of honest vehicles increases, adding attackers will change rapidly the density from fluid to congested.

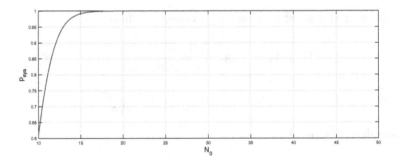

Fig. 1. Sybil attack probability vs N_0

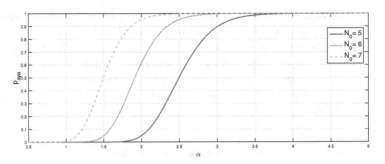

Fig. 2. Sybil attack probability vs α

6   Conclusion

This paper presents a new Sybil attack detection mechanism for VANETs. This mechanism considers each vehicle, as a Cooperative-Intelligent Transportation System Station, exchanging CAM messages. It takes advantage from a well-known macroscopic traffic flow models, that are supposed to be already provided to the vehicles. We first presented an algorithm that detects the Sybil attack using the CAM messages provided by neighbours. This algorithm allows to estimate the speed of the vehicle using the fundamental diagram of the road's segment. If this estimated speed is too different from the real one, it detects an attack and broadcasts an alert to other nodes. Once the attack is detected, the trigger node waits for a confirmation from its neighbours in order to consider it as an attack and not a false detection one. This mechanism which is easy to be implemented and very powerful has been also validated through a mathematical model and some numerical simulations that prove its.

Our future works will deal with the identification of the attackers and the design of some countermeasures to fight against them.

Acknowledgement. This work was made possible by EC Grant No. INEA/CEF/ TRAN/A2014/1042281 from the INEA Agency for the SCOOP project. The statements made herein are solely the responsibility of the authors.

References

1. Al-Sultan, S., Al-Doori, M.M., Al-Bayatti, A.H., Zedan, H.: A comprehensive survey on vehicular Ad Hoc network. J. Netw. Comput. Appl. **31**(37), 380–92 (2014)
2. Maxwell, J.C.: A Treatise on Electricity and Magnetism, 3rd edn, vol. 2, pp. 68–73. Clarendon, Oxford (1892)
3. Newsome, J., Shi, E., Song, D., Perrig, A.: The sybil attack in sensor networks: analysis defenses. In: Proceedings of International Symposium on Information Processing in Sensor Networks, pp. 259–268 (2004)
4. Pal, S., Mukhopadhyay, A.K., Bhattacharya, P.P.: Defending mechanisms against sybil attack in next generation mobile ad hoc networks. IETE Tech. Rev. **25**(4), 209–214 (2008)
5. Raya, M., Hubaux, J.P.: Securing vehicular ad hoc networks. J. Comput. Secur. Spec. Issue Secur. Ad Hoc Sens. Netw. **15**(1), 3968 (2007)
6. Raya, M., Papadimitratos, P., Hubaux, J.P.: Securing vehicular communications. IEEE Wirel. Commun. Mag. Spec. Issue InterVehicular Commun. **13**(5), 815 (2006)
7. Study on the Deployment of C-ITS in Europe: Final Report. https://ec.europa.eu/ transport/sites/transport/files/2016-c-its-deployment-study-final-report.pdf
8. Garip, M.T., Reiher, P., Gerla, M.: Ghost: concealing vehicular botnet communication in the VANET control channel. In: 2016 International Wireless Communications and Mobile Computing Conference (IWCMC), Paphos, pp. 1–6 (2016). https://doi. org/10.1109/IWCMC.2016.7577024
9. Zeroual, A., Messai, N., Kechida, S., Hamdi, F.: A piecewise switched linear approach for traffic flow modeling. Int. J. Autom. Comput. **14**, 729–741 (2017)

Intelligent Transport System Based on Bluetooth

Kévin Thomas[✉], Hacène Fouchal, Stephane Cormier, and Francis Rousseaux

CReSTIC, Université de Reims Champagne-Ardenne, Reims, France
{Kevin.Thomas,Hacene.Fouchal,Stephane.Cormier,
Francis.Rousseaux}@univ-reims.fr

Abstract. A Cooperative Intelligent Transport System (C-ITS) is a system where mobile stations OBU (On-Board Units) exchange messages with other ITSS-V (Intelligent Transport System Station Vehicle) or RSU (Road Side Units). Messages are sent through a specific WIFI (IEEE 802.11p) denoted also ETSI ITS-G5. The efficiency of this technology has been proven in terms of latency. However, RSU are common everywhere and stations equipped with G5 interface are not widely deployed. For this reason we look for another mean to guarantee this communication. Bluetooth Low Energy (BLE) is deployed on smartphones. We take advantage of this deployment to propose an architecture based on this protocol in order to build a Cooperative Intelligent Transport System. Cellular networks are widely deployed and can support these communications. We have adapted the ITS stack provided by the ETSI (designed for G5) to the BLE protocol.

Keywords: C-ITS · VANETs · Cellular networks ·
Hybrid communications · BLE

1 Introduction

The deployment of connected vehicles is an interesting challenge since a decade. The connectivity is one of the most important issue to solve. Indeed, a dedicated WIFI has been designed for connected vehicles: IEEE 802.11p (denoted also ETSI ITS-G5). However, the deployment of ITS-G5 hotspots (denoted Road Side Units) is not generalised. This deployment of such technology takes a lot of time and is an expensive task. Indeed, the penetration rate of the connected vehicles is increasing slowly. Therefore, the coverage of such technology remains limited. However, it is very important to receive the events to avoid accidents and save lives. To deal with this, the coverage could be enhanced using the BLE protocol. In this paper, we intend to use Bluetooth protocol for the delivery of warning messages to and from vehicles. Every vehicles send continuously it Cooperative Awareness Messages (CAM) to the Central ITS Station (ITSS-C, or *National C-ITS Station*). The latter maintains the location of the vehicles up-to-date. If an event is triggered in an area, a Decentralized Event Notification

© Springer Nature Switzerland AG 2019
B. Hilt et al. (Eds.): Nets4Cars/Nets4Trains/Nets4Aircraft 2019, LNCS 11461, pp. 50–59, 2019.
https://doi.org/10.1007/978-3-030-25529-9_5

Message (DENM) is then automatically forwarded to the nodes that are in the relevance area.

The remainder of this paper is organised as follows: Sect. 2 describes the related works. Section 3 details the architecture of the proposed system. Then, Sect. 4 and Sect. 5 presents the Vehicle to Infrastructure communication and the Vehicle to Vehicle communication. Finally, Sect. 6 concludes the paper and gives some hints about future works.

2 Related Works

[13] proposes an evaluation of vehicular communications networks through car sharing scenarios. The authors have investigated three parameters. They adopted a specific mobility model which has been imported to a simulator. They have worked on a grid Manhattan network and they observed some performance parameters such as delay, packet loss, etc. The most important objective of the study is to show that vehicular communication is feasible and realistic under some conditions.

[12] studies throughput over VANETs system along an unidirectional traffic for different conditions and transmission ranges of wireless equipments. All studied vehicles are randomly connected. The paper gives few results of simulation studies achieved on NS-2 toolbox. They have measured performances indicators in case of congestion. A comparison of the obtained results with the expected connectivity has been done and have shown that the throughput over simulation is lower due to packet losses caused by collisions.

Authors of [19] presents an alternative to WAVE/DSRC using an hybrid system, which uses Wi-Fi Direct and Cellular Network. They show that such a system could work for C-ITS. However, this paper does not take into account the hybridation between ITS-G5 and Cellular Network.

[20] presents another alternative to WAVE/DSRC solution using here Wi-Fi Direct, ZigBee and Cellular Network. Wi-Fi Direct is used as a direct link between nodes. ZigBee is used to connect roadside sensors and Cellular Network for long distance communication. In this study, the ITS-G5 is also ignored.

In [7], the authors provide their network architecture which has been deployed in Spain, where communicating vehicles are switching between 802.11p and 3G, depending on RSU's availability.

[15] presents a detailed study on performance evaluation of IEEE 80211.p networks versus LTE vehicular networks. The authors analyzed some performance indicators like the end-to-end delay for both networks in different scenarios (high density, urban environments, etc.). Many important issues have been measured as network availability and reliability. The authors have proved through simulations that LTE solution meets most of the application requirements in terms of reliability, scalability, and mobility. However, IEEE 802.11p provides acceptable performance for sparse network topologies with limited mobility support.

[17] gives an efficient solution for routing messages over VANETs by using the vehicle's heading.

[6] gives an overview of how research on vehicular communication evolved in Europe and, especially, in Germany. They describe the German field operational test sim TD. The project sim TD is the first field operational test that evaluated the effectiveness and benefits of applications based on vehicular communication in a setup that is representative for a realistic deployment environment. It is, therefore, the next necessary step to prepare for an informed deployment decision of cooperative systems.

[16] is dedicated to routing over VANETs in an urban environment. [14] is a study about movement prediction of vehicles. Indeed, an adapted routing algorithms are proposed in [10] and in [11]. [9] gives an overview of strategies to use for routing on VANETs. [18] reviews much more actual strategies on vehicular networks.

All the works presented below handle the communication between vehicles using cellular networks or ETSI ITS-G5 networks. There is no approach about the Bluetooth Communication, technology massively used in advertising or home automation, etc ...

3   Proposed Architecture

3.1   Environment

This architecture intends to provide another type of communication in Cooperative Intelligent Transport System (C-ITS) project. This model uses the Bluetooth technology and more precisely the Bluetooth Low Energy (BLE) advertise data.

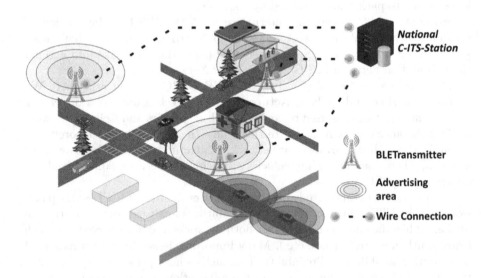

Fig. 1. Global BLE architecture

As we can see in Fig. 1, some BLE antennas, denoted BLETransmitters, are dispatched on the road, and connected to the *National C-ITS Station* which controls them. They broadcast information and listen to messages which come from vehicles driving around. However, some BLE On Board Units are installed in vehicles, they can also broadcast information and listen to messages which come from other vehicles or BLETransmitters.

3.2 Messages Format

A Cooperative Awarness message (CAM) and Decentralized Environmental Notification Message (DENM) are described by the ETSI Standard C-ITS. The objective of this kind of messages is, respectively, broadcast the vehicle's position with other information which concern the vehicle's structure and announces events on the road. Here we will use a light version of this kind of messages. We intend to be compatible with Bluetooth 4.x and 5. We are limited to 31 bytes on an advertise message's payload.

Light CAM. We define the following packet structure. This allows to respect the size limit and to upload all required geographic information to the server to locate the vehicle.

0	1	2	3	4	5	6	7	8	9	10	11	12	13	14	15	16	17	18	19	20	21	22	23
MT	Station ID			Lat			Long			H	GDT			Security									

In this structure, we have:

- *Message Type (MT)* - To identify if it is a light CAM or a light DENM.
- *Station ID* - This is the vehicle's pseudonym, it allows to identify the vehicle and protects its privacy. Indeed this pseudonym changes every 5 min according to privacy requirements.
- *Latitude/Longitude* - The GPS location.
- *Heading (H)* - It is the angle between the vehicle's direction and the North. This information is necessary to identify the lane where the vehicle is.
- *Generation Delta Time (GDT)* - The build time of the message, necessary for event management on the National C-ITS-Station.

Light DENM. Here we define the light packet for an event, a light DENM. However we distinguish two kind of light DENM: "light DENM declaration" and "light DENM targeted".

We first define the structure of the message to be sent to the National C-ITS-Station (communication Vehicle To Infrastructure: see Sect. 3) or to an other vehicle (communication Vehicle to Vehicle: see Sect. 4):

0	1	2	3	4	5	6	7	8	9	10	11	12	13	14	15	16	17	18	19	20
MT	DC	Lat			Long			H	T		Security									

In this structure, we have:

- *Message Type (MT)* - To identify if it is a light CAM or a light DENM.
- *DENM Code (DC)* - Event Code maps from the ITS CauseCode/SubCauseCode Table.

- *Latitude/Longitude* - The GPS location.
- *Heading (H)* - It is the angle between the vehicle's direction and the North. This information is necessary to identify the lane where the vehicle is.
- *Timestamp (T)* -   mod 2^{16} of the ITS timestamp. The build time of the message, necessary to determine the validity duration of the event.

Here we define the message to be received from the National Central Station.

0	1	2	3	4	5	6	7	8	9	10	11	12	13	14	15
MT	Station ID				HL	DC		Lat				Long			
H	T		VD			Security									

In this structure, we have:

- *Message Type (MT)* - To identify if it is a light CAM or a light DENM.
- *Station ID* - It allows to identify the vehicle targeted by the message.
- *Hop Limit (HL)* - Number of hop which can be done by the denm. Foreach hop, the value is decremented.
- *DENM Code (DC)* - Event Code maps from the ITS CauseCode/SubCauseCode Table.
- *Latitude/Longitude* - The GPS location.
- *Heading (H)* - It is the angle between the vehicle's direction and the North. This information is necessary to identify the lane where the vehicle is.
- *Timestamp (T)* -   mod 2^{16} of the ITS timestamp. The build time of the message, necessary to determine the validity duration of the event.
- *Validity Duration (VD)* - life time of the event.

So, in this part, we have seen which infrastructures are necessary to provide this new type of communication for C-ITS Stations, and which messages can be exchanged according to size limits of the BLE.

4   Vehicle to Infrastructure Communication

As we can see in Fig. 2, (1) a vehicle broadcasts its BLE message. It can be a light CAM or a light DENM but in this example, we consider that it is a light CAM. (2) This one is received by the BLETransmitter which forwards this message to the National C-ITS-Station thanks to wire connection (3). (4) The National C-ITS-Station has the location of the vehicle, determines what are information which concerns it and forwards information to BLETransmitter (5) which are on the potential path of reach it. This one requires an analysis of the cartography. Then BLETransmitter advertises information for the vehicle (6) during the validity duration's event.

For a DENM upload from the vehicle, it is more or less the same process, we just do not have the step (5) and (6) because the vehicle already knows this event.

Let us focus on the step (4) the National C-ITS-Station process.

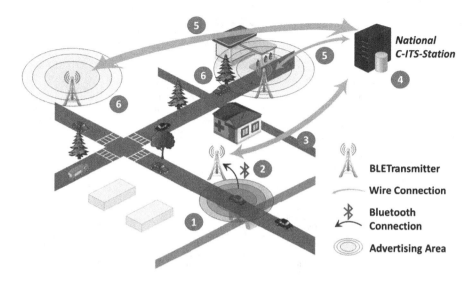

Fig. 2. Vehicle to infrastructure communication

Figure 3 shows income information on the National C-ITS-Station. When the vehicle moves on the Road, it can send some CAMs or DENMs according to the Fig. 2. After that a message is received by a BLETransmitter and forwards to the National C-ITS-Station, the message is decoded. Its geographic position is identified. Then 2 options are available:

- The message is a *light CAM*: if the station ID of the vehicle is already known, the position is updated. If the station ID is unknown, a new Mobile Node manager is started. Then the routine is run.
- The message is a *light DENM*: it is localized on a cartography and, corresponding to its event code, a relevance distance is applied on it. Then it is stored on the DENMs Database. If the DENM is already known, the message is discarded.

Now how the process works? We are based on the process describes in [21].

As we can see in Fig. 4, for each iteration, two process are engaged onto the Mobile Node Manager:

- picks the last position and last heading of the vehicle to identify DENM(s) which concerns our vehicle. If some DENMs are identified, they are saved in local database and been prepared to the sending.
- picks the last position and last heading of the vehicle to analyse the cartography and identifies what are BLETransmitters which will be on the way of the vehicle.

When DENMs must be sent and BLETransmitters are identified, the *National C-ITS Station* commands the start advertising of the information. Then the Mobile Node Manager waits the next light CAM received from the vehicle.

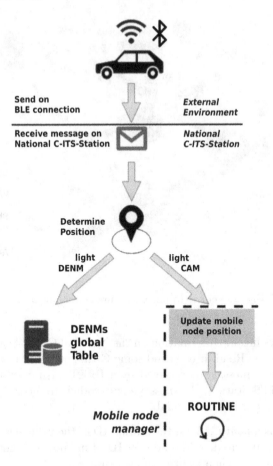

Fig. 3. Messages incoming on National C-ITS-Station.

So, in this section, we have seen how the vehicle is managed on the *National C-ITS Station* and how information are identified and sent to the vehicle concerned. We have based our approach on [21] for the Mobile Node Manager on the *National C-ITS Station*, it is slightly the same process, we have just provided another communication protocol.

5   Vehicle to Vehicle Communication

This architecture also allows to transmit some DENMs to other vehicles.

Here, Fig. 5 shows (1) where the vehicle notifies a new event (2) if another vehicle is in the advertise area, (3) the vehicle, which follows, will receive the message and add the event to its database. If the DENM is already known, the message is discarded.

This Section shows that this architecture can also provide communication between vehicles. This feature is very limited by senders devices (the sending

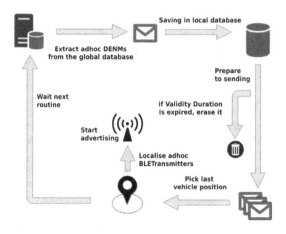

Fig. 4. Sending process on Mobile node manager on National C-ITS-Station.

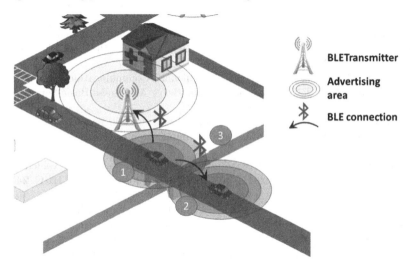

Fig. 5. Vehicle to Vehicle communication

area is very limited in BLE for smartphone or other Class 2 Bluetooth Chip) but it provides a good alternative for ITS G5 vehicle to vehicle communication.

6   Conclusion

In this paper we have presented an architecture for intelligent transport system based on the bluetooth protocol. The most important issue of such a study is to show that a simple protocol could be used very simply with low cost to deploy Cooperative Intelligent Transport Systems. We have only presented an architecture et as a next step we intend to experiment such a solution on real vehicles within the project SCOOP (supported by the EC).

Acknowledgement. This work was made possible by EC Grant No. INEA/CEF/ TRAN/A2014/1042281 from the INEA Agency for the SCOOP project. The statements made herein are solely the responsibility of the authors.

References

1. European Telecommunications Standards Institute (ETSI). http://www.etsi.org
2. IEEE Draft Standard for Amendment to Standard [for] Information Technology-Telecommunications and information exchange between systems-Local and Metropolitan networks-Specific requirements-Part II: Wireless LAN Medium Access Control (MAC) and Physical Layer (PHY) specifications-Amendment 6: Wireless Access in Vehicular Environments, in IEEE Std P802.11p/D11.0 April 2010, pp. 1–35, 15 June 2010
3. Intelligent Transport Systems (ITS); Vehicular Communications; GeoNetworking; Part 4: Geographical addressing and forwarding for point-to-point and point-to-multipoint communications; Sub-part 1: Media-Independent Functionality. ETSI EN 302 636-4-1 V1.2.1, July 2014
4. Intelligent Transport Systems (ITS); Vehicular Communications; GeoNetworking; Part 5: Transport Protocols; Sub-part 1: Basic Transport Protocol. ETSI EN 302 636-5-1 V1.2.1, August 2014
5. Intelligent Transport Systems (ITS); Vehicular Communications; Basic Set of Applications; Part 2: Specification of Cooperative Awareness Basic Service. ETSI EN 302 637–2 vol 1.3.2, November 2014
6. Weia, C.: V2X communication in Europe: from research projects towards standardisation and field testing of vehicle communication technology. Comput. Netw. **55**(14), 3103–3119 (2011)
7. Santa, J., Fernandez, P.J., Perenaguez-Garcia, F.: Deployment of vehicular networks in highways using 802.11p and IPv6 technologies. Int. JAHUC **24**(1/2), 33–48 (2017)
8. Intelligent Transport Systems (ITS); Vehicular Communications; Basic Set of Applications; Part 3: Specifications of Decentralized Environmental Notification Basic Service. ETSI EN 302 637–3 V1.2.2, November 2014
9. Lochert, C., Hartenstein, H., Tian, J., Fussler, H., Hermann, D., Mauve, M.: A routing strategy for vehicular ad hoc networks in city environments. In: IEEE IV2003 Intelligent Vehicles Symposium. Proceedings (Cat. No. 03TH8683), pp. 156–161, June 2003
10. Ayaida, M., Barhoumi, M., Fouchal, H., Ghamri-Doudane, Y., Afilal, L.: PHRHLS: a movement-prediction-based joint routing and hierarchical location service for Vanets. In: IEEE International Conference on Communications (ICC), Budapest, Hungary, pp. 1424–1428, May 2013
11. Ayaida, M., Barhoumi, M., Fouchal, H., Ghamri-Doudane, Y., Afilal, L.: HHLS: a hybrid routing technique for VANETs. In: Global Communications Conference (GLOBECOM), Anaheim, pp. 44–48. IEEE, December 2012
12. Lu, W., Bao, Y., Sun, X., Wang, Z.: Performance evaluation of inter-vehicle communication in a unidirectional dynamic traffic flow with shockwave. In: Proceedings of the International Conference on Ultra Modern Telecommunications, ICUMT 2009, 12–14 October 2009, St. Petersburg, Russia, pp. 1–6 (2009)
13. Lu, W., Han, L.D., Cherry, C.R.: Evaluation of vehicular communication networks in a car sharing system. Int. J. Intell. Transp. Syst. Res. **11**(3), 113–119 (2013)

14. Menouar, H., Lenardi, M., Filali, F.: A movement prediction-based routing protocol for vehicle-to-vehicle communications. In V2VCOM, : 1st International Vehicle-to-Vehicle Communications Workshop, co-located with MobiQuitous 2005, 21 July 2005, San Diego, USA, San Diego, USA, July 2005

15. Mir, Z.H., Filali, F.: LTE and IEEE 802.11p for vehicular networking: a performance evaluation. EURASIP J. Wirel. Commun. Netw. 89 (2014)

16. Seet, B.-C., Liu, G., Lee, B.-S., Foh, C.-H., Wong, K.-J., Lee, K.-K.: A-STAR: a mobile Ad Hoc routing strategy for metropolis vehicular communications. In: Mitrou, N., Kontovasilis, K., Rouskas, G.N., Iliadis, I., Merakos, L. (eds.) NETWORKING 2004. LNCS, vol. 3042, pp. 989–999. Springer, Heidelberg (2004). https://doi.org/10.1007/978-3-540-24693-0_81

17. Taleb, T., Ochi, M., Jamalipour, A., Kato, N., Nemoto, Y.: An efficient vehicle-heading based routing protocol for VANET networks. In: Wireless Communications and Networking Conference, WCNC 2006, vol. 4, pp. 2199–2204. IEEE, April 2006

18. Zeadally, S., Hunt, R., Chen, Y.-S., Irwin, A., Hassan, A.: Vehicular ad hoc networks (VANETS): status, results, and challenges. Telecommun. Syst. 50(4), 217–241 (2012)

19. Jeong, S., Baek, Y., Son, S.H.: A hybrid V2X system for safety-critical applications in VANET. In: 2016 IEEE 4th International Conference on Cyber-Physical Systems, Networks, and Applications (CPSNA), Nagoya, pp. 13–18 (2016)

20. Bhover, S.U., Tugashetti, A., Rashinkar, P.: V2X communication protocol in VANET for co-operative intelligent transportation system. In: International Conference on Innovative Mechanisms for Industry Applications (ICIMIA), Bangalore, pp. 602–607 (2017)

21. Wilhelm, G., Fouchal, H., Thomas, K., Ayaida, M.: A C-ITS central station as a communication manager. In: International Conference on Innovations for Community Services 2018 (I4CS 2018), Zilina, pp. 33–43 (2018)

Linkage of IoT Technologies with the SWE (SOS) Standard for the Development of a Heterogeneous Intelligent Transport System (Case Study Quito)

Ana Zambrano[1], Eduardo Ortiz M.[1], Marcelo Zambrano[2],
Xavier Calderón[1], and Luis Urquiza-Aguiar[1(✉)] 🆔

[1] Departamento de Telecomunicaciones y Redes de Información,
Escuela Politécnica Nacional, Quito 170525, Ecuador
{ana.zambrano,eduardo.ortiz,xavier.calderon,
luis.urquiza}@epn.edu.ec
[2] Carrera de Ingeniería en Telecomunicaciones, Universidad Técnica del Norte,
Ibarra 100110, Ecuador
omzambrano@utn.edu.ec

Abstract. Transport plays a fundamental role in the economic development for big cities. Quito, the capital of Ecuador, presents serious mobility problems, with a significant amount of traffic both in the city center and in its main access roads. The detailed proposal in this article aims to link Quito with several new generation technologies such as *Internet of Things (Iot)*, *Sensor Web Enablement (SWE)* standard for heterogeneous sensor communication, and a system of real-time notifications using the communications protocol *Message Queue Telemetry Transport (MQTT)*. These technologies will be used for the development of an Intelligent Transport System (ITS) that takes advantage of the massive deployment of smartphones in the society as main sources of information, including *Arduino* and *Raspberry* modules to check efficient communication. This ITS bases its operation on the paradigm of the *Crowdsensing*, which allows to reflect more accurately the reality of the object of study when more collaborators use the system; reaching up to 30% improvement in the situational consciousness of the environment variable, the traffic.

Keywords: Internet of Things · Sensor Web Enablement ·
Message Queue Telemetry Transport · Intelligent Transport System ·
Crowdsensing

1 Introduction

Currently, one critical problem affecting Quito is urban mobility [1] as it has not been properly managed and planned when designing the city. Indeed, this problem is so serious that has caused several economical, cultural and even health problems among inhabitants (stress and fatigue of drivers). As a result, Quito has demonstrated to have a slow growth in development in its infrastructure and quality of life standards.

© Springer Nature Switzerland AG 2019
B. Hilt et al. (Eds.): Nets4Cars/Nets4Trains/Nets4Aircraft 2019, LNCS 11461, pp. 60–69, 2019.
https://doi.org/10.1007/978-3-030-25529-9_6

This is demonstrated by statistics showing considerable growth of the automotive park in recent years [2], the import of vehicles in 2016 was 31,761 units and 70,203 in 2017 respectively [3]; this data shows a growth of more than 121% compared to 2016. Likewise, vehicle sales for 2017 [4] present an increase of more than 65% with respect to 2016 [5]. This incremental growth impacts on society due to the lack of proper vehicular planning and management systems. As a result, many products and services cannot be delivered. There is not available in Ecuador, an Intelligent Transport System (ITS) [6] that combines the benefits of existing information systems and tools, such that people in the society can be aware about transportation conditions in real-time. Thus, citizens rely on social networks mostly to be aware about incidents in the traffic. Unfortunately, this information tends to be mostly inaccurate and unreliable.

To counter these issues, in this paper, we propose the development and design of an ITS that mitigates the problem of urban mobility. We implement a prototype and use Quito as case study. Our ITS allows the distribution of information in real time about the state of traffic in the different road rings of the city, both in terms of incidents raised in the tracks, as well as different types of information relevant to the drivers can improve their situational awareness and make appropriate decisions (available pathways, derivations, jams, etc.). The prototype presents a distributed architecture of communications that makes it possible to obtain information from any type of devices, either a smartphone, *Raspberry* or *Arduino* devices and more. This heterogeneity has allowed to implement *Sensor Web Enablement* (*SWE*) standard in particular its main component *Sensor Observation Service* (*SOS*).

The heterogeneity achieved delivers as an advantage, being able to cover extensive geographical areas as in the case of Quito at almost zero cost, taking advantage of community sensors. As a group *SWE* and *SOS*, the master protocol IoT [7], *Message Queue Telemetry Transport* (*MQTT*) [8] is used, this one manages the sending/receiving of messages in real time, benefiting the architecture with its low energy consumption, bandwidth, and processing capacity within the devices where it is hosted. This provides useful information for drivers to prevent or avoid massive delays in displacement, excessive fuel consumption, increases in greenhouse gases, failure to schedule [9]. With the development of this system is intended to improve the effective mobility of people, merchandise and even aid bodies, with the ultimate goal of contributing positively to the wellbeing and development of communities.

This article is divided as follows. Section 2 discusses the related work regarding frameworks that solve the mobility problem of big cities. The proposed architecture is then presented in Sect. 3, where we describe the system's action scenario, as well as the role played by each of the technologies employed. Next in Sect. 4, the detail of the features of the mobile application is presented with its respective analysis of results. In the light of our results, we present a discussion in Sect. 5. Lastly, we present our conclusions and future work in Sect. 6.

2 Related Work

ITS is a new proposal to reduce the impact of transportation-related problems in large cities. To mitigate these problems, ITS propose the development of computer systems oriented to efficient transport management, integrating in a single system vehicles, technology and road infrastructure, mobile devices and society [10]. One of the most relevant examples of ITS is in Michigan USA, called "ItsMichigan" [11]. It has a system of video cameras and adaptive traffic lights for the optimization and control of traffic within the city. In Moscow Russia [12], the authorities of vehicular adminis-tration have implemented an adaptive traffic system called "ITS-Russia". This system uses sensors of vehicle presence and radars of photo detection in open sky to discover incidents in Road as vehicles unprepared or in the opposite direction, among others. On the other hand, in Ambato Ecuador [13] in certain avenues, vehicle counting cameras were installed along with an artificial vision system [14]. Obviously, this implies a great investment by the authorities and it is known that these systems were relegated to abandonment due to lack of resources, common problem in developing countries. Another problem to mention is that the results of these systems are not disseminated to the citizenry so that it can plan and make decisions about their mobility, forcing it to organize through social networks that although widely used, are not a reliable source of information and often information is often decontextualized and untimely.

This article presents an ITS-Quito, which is part of the Ecuador Intelligent Roads project (E-iRoads), whose main objective is to improve the situational awareness of the transport routes of a city, for the timely making of decisions in developing cities, such as Quito, whose budget is reduced. It is intended that this solution be a feasible and economic ITS for any city, which takes advantage of the large deployment of smart-phones in the citizenry as the main source of sensors. For example, it contemplates the development of an opportunistic mobile application [15], that takes advantage of any type of heterogeneous sensor (like smartphones of any characteristics and SO), both for the visualization of results and for the compilation of data respectively.

To allow the communication of all these heterogeneous sensors, the Sensor Observation Service (SOS) component, belonging to SWE, standard was implemented. The SOS is a web interface for data collection and consultation that defines interop-erability interfaces for the coding of the metadata obtained by each of the system sensors. The objective is to increase the number of sensors and to analyze the data obtained to get *Crowdsensing*, which is a technique that involves a large number of people with mobile devices capable of measuring data of a common interest. These data are shared collectively to improve or predict any processes. In addition, as the number of users increases [16], the data will be described with greater veracity of the object of study.

On the other hand, users benefit from real-time notifications, through the protocol MQTT [17]. The integration of these technologies allows, at an almost null cost, unlike the aforementioned projects, create a real situational and timely awareness in the dri-vers, which in turn allows improving the decision-making. In addition, this proposal exceeds projects such as [11, 13] by granting the ability to incorporate heterogeneous sensors and can cover large territories.

3   Architecture

Before The proposed system, consisting of three main blocks, is detailed in Fig. 1. This system is formed, in the first instance, by the "Information Source Block" which represents a set of sampling devices for the collection of data. It also includes the development of a mobile application for sampling. The "Sensor Block" is an implementation of the SWE standard; in particular, the Sensor Observation System (SOS) component is used to implement an interface through a web service, with the objective of obtaining information in the form of observations and the sensor descriptions. Moreover, the "Notification Block", that uses the MQTT protocol that represents a channel dedicated to the circulation of incident messages for notification to carriers. In summary, the MQTT protocol is used for the implementation of a real-time notification system and the HTTP protocol, for sending the data to the SWE-SOS web interface. There is no geographical limit for the use of this system, because the server is reachable through the Web. The Union of these three blocks forms the ITS described.

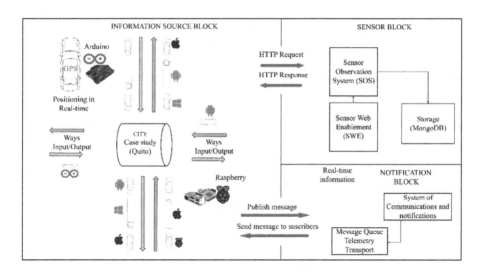

Fig. 1. Technical block of the system.

For this research smartphones, Arduino and Raspberry modules have been used as source of information. This data is part of the SWE-SOS standard message that is sent in JSON format to the server to be stored in the database. All devices (smartphones, Arduino and Raspberry) are responsible for measuring their own vehicle's travel speed. To achieve this goal, first, a mobile application has been developed that obtains geographic locations (double) through the GPS sensor, and determines its velocity. This data is obtained periodically (sampling frequency = 2 min) and then is sent to the server. In addition, this application has the ability to connect to the MQTT server to send or receive incident messages from the route (String) which are sent manually by the end users. Second, devices as Arduino Uno [18] and Raspberry Pi 3 [19], together with a GPS module (GY-GPS6MV2 [20]) has been added to perform the vehicle's location in order to obtain its velocity. In addition, a GSM module (GSM 900 [21, 22]) has been added to both devices to send the data to the remote server through the Web. These devices, which can be smartphones, Arduino or Raspberry, were installed in the vehicle cabin to perform sensorization tasks and notify drivers. It is important to note that the energy necessary for the operation of these devices has been obtained from the vehicle power output. For example, for an Arduino, first in the laboratory the components have been assembled, which are the GPS module, and the GSM module. Then the functionalities have been codified, which are the sensing of the speed of the vehicle and notification in real time. Finally, these physical components have been installed in the vehicle verifying their autonomy and correct operation.

The tools that allowed developing this proposal were a non-relational database service *MongoDb* for the storage of the measured information of the route to study and the description of the sensors. The PHP programming language was used to make the web interface achievable for heterogeneous clients. To implement the alert notification system, the MQTT Eclipse Mosquitto Broker server has been used. These components, with the exception of the mobile client, are hosted on a host with Ubuntu server 16.04 LTS operating system, which is instantiated on the VMware ESXi virtualization platform of a physical server at the Escuela Politécnica Nacional [23] with a public IP accessible through the Web [24]. The Fig. 2a shows the integration of all these technologies for the implementation of the system, where it is observed that the main source of information is a set of heterogeneous devices. It is worth mentioning that the standard establishes the guidelines for communication and messages. The *SWE-SOS* defines six messages to achieve a heterogeneous web interface: *insertObservation, getObservation, insertSensor, deleteSensor, updateSensor, getCapabilities* [25]. For example, for the entry of new data to the server, the *insertObservation* operation must be implemented as shown in Fig. 2b. This operation is a JSON message that flows from the heterogeneous client to the server. The message shown in Fig. 2b, contains the main value of the measurement (velocity) and the metadata that allow identifying: the standard version, the type of query, route identifiers, the geographical location of the data, the date and time in the fact that the data was taken.

The mobile application allows the visualization of the analysis of the data found in the *MongoDb* database. In addition, the mobile application allows to know using spatial and temporal filters the average velocity and the arrival time. For example, the data corresponding to the velocity are analyzed to show to the end user the average velocity and the possible delay in the route. On the other hand, an interactive map presents the geographical location of the user and the incidents reported by other users in a period of time in order to improve situational awareness.

4   Preliminary Results

For the validation of the system, we had the collaboration of FENATRAPE (National Federation of Heavy Transport of Ecuador) that facilitated agreements with companies of heavy transport for the design of the scenario and the validation of the developed system. The stage was kept in each company for the time of a month getting promising

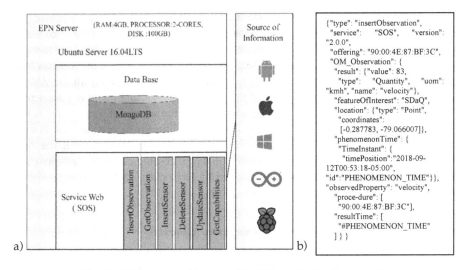

Fig. 2. (a) System architecture. (b) SOS standard code example.

results and welcome. Taking into account that the vehicles where the driver does not have a smartphone, an Arduino or a Raspberry prototype have been installed. The mobile application in the areas of average consumption of the battery in mw, has been evaluated, and the use of the CPU compared to applications known as WhatsApp y Messenger, to discard possible causes of uninstallation which can reduce the *Crowdsensing* damaging the system. These results are observed in the Fig. 3.

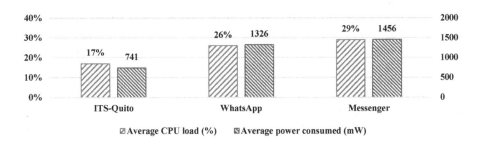

Fig. 3. ITS-Quito comparison with known social applications.

It has been performed a series of tests in different places in the city, where it was evident the improvement of the situational consciousness by 30% through a survey of 65 volunteer carriers. This means that at least 18 people made a better decision based on the information provided by this system. Even so, some of them did not go on a trip when observing accidents or work on the road; other drivers took alternating routes when observing that on the route there was intense traffic. These volunteers indicated (in the survey) that this information was not obtained by any other applications. In this way it is able to optimize the decision making in the planning of trips, reducing the traffic as a consequence. Likewise, the *Crowdsensing* was reaffirmed because the results shown to the carriers improve considerably by increasing the number of users.

In turn, it has validated the performance of the server along with all its tools to corroborate its design. First, the server hosts the Web interface, which implements *SOS* operations for heterogeneous clients. This interface has been tested with the *JMeter* software to evaluate the average in *ms* of the service requests, among other parameters. The results show that even for 10000 samples/requests the average response time is less than 1 s, verifying its character in Real Time. In addition, it is emphasized that no errors were presented in the applications made. These results show that the *SOS* interface implemented has a large amount of data processing capacity, sufficient and necessary for a large number of sensors addressing large cities such as Quito, as shown in Table 1.

Table 1. Load the server test results.

Samples	Average (ms)	Min (ms)	Max (min)	Received KB/sec
100	355	261	531	30,92
1000	466	267	951	37,73
10000	698	265	1159	35,59

5 Discussion

According to the results obtained, this section is presented to show the benefits and drawbacks of the heterogeneous ITS to Quito city developed, as well as the criteria used to solve the difficulties.

According to the results of the mobile application, it was observed that the consumption of the host's hardware resources was not significant, and even less than social mobile applications known as *WhatsApp* among others. However, these results may vary by altering the frequency of data sampling of the route. If the frequency would increase, the mobile application would consume more resources such as CPU, battery, RAM, and bandwidth. Which can cause the uninstallation of the application affecting the *Crowdsensing*. On the other hand, by decreasing the frequency the system would not have enough data to emit relevant results for users. In this sense, these criteria must be taken into account for every system in real time. Consequently, a balance must be found to avoid stressing mobile devices without losing the amount of data necessary for the system.

Our research, in contradistinction to projects such as ITS-Michigan or ITS-Russia provides a solution to the Quito community at low cost, that is, it does not require a large technological deployment which obviously will require a large economic investment, this is not feasible for countries in the process of development like Ecuador. Smartphones are the main source of information; first the data collection and second, for the publication of results. Allowing everyone with a smartphone to be part of the system.

Crowdsensing has been measured in a scalable way. That is, users have been progressively added to the system to observe its technical behavior. As shown in Table 2, the forecast time provided by the system has been compared with the actual travel time to measure the efficiency of the system. The trend in this table indicates that the greater the number of users, the system data is closer to reality.

Table 2. Comparison of real time with delay time (Application).

Number of users	Real time (min)	Forecast time (Application) (min)	Error rate (%)
10	186	167	10,21%
30	170	155	8,82%
60	189	175	7,40%

A problem to mention in the research could be in terms of security. First, to send sensor data to the server, sensors must register in the system following the standard SWE-SOS. Later, in order to achieve the results of the route, the identification of the sensors is revealed, which can cause vulnerabilities in the system. A possible solution could be, the encryption of the identification of the sensors to avoid attacks due to insecurity.

6   Conclusions and Future Work

Population and vehicular growth in large cities must go hand in and out of the improvement of transport management systems. In Quito Ecuador drivers experience hours of delay due to the amount of traffic in the city. This article presents the prototype for an Intelligent Traffic System (ITS) that allows to notify in real time to the drivers about any incident provoked in the pathways, and in general way, of the state of traffic in the whole city. In this way, the drivers acquire a real and timely situational awareness that allows them to make appropriate decisions and in time.

The proposed architecture envisions the implementation of a system of notifications in real time, by means of the Protocol of Communications *MQTT*, whose performance has been paramount to multiplex the channel of communications in several subchannels, same that represent each of the access roads to the city of Quito. On the other hand, the data on the state of the pathways are measured and provided by different types of heterogeneous sensors (smartphones, *Arduino, Raspberry*), i.e. the system has the ability to accept as customers any type of sensor that can measure a route parameter and send this result through the web. These data have been modeled according to the guidelines of the *SWE - SOS* standard.

In the future, it is considered to incorporate new technologies for the visualization of the system data as a *SPA* (*Single Page Application*) that allows to experiment in a fluent way the data obtained from the mobile clients, because these data are dynamic and vary after a time interval. In addition, it provides for the implementation of other features of the *MQTT* protocol such as the media hierarchy and the connection with remote servers *MQTT*, to avoid possible points of failure of the developed system.

Acknowledgment. Authors gratefully acknowledge the financial support provided by the Escuela Politécnica Nacional, for the development of the project PIJ-15-20 "E-iRoads: Ecuador - Inteligent Roads. Un Sistema inteligente para la gestión de tráfico en las periferias de grandes ciudades (Caso de Estudio: Quito)".

References

1. Freire Mullo, J.E., Nájera Puente, J.F.: Estudio de movilidad en la ciudad de Quito en horarios pico, utilizando datos móviles de la empresa telefónica, Ecuador (2017)
2. AEADE: Sector automotor en cifras. http://www.aeade.net/wp-content/uploads/2018/03/boletin%2018%20espanol%20resumido.pdf
3. SENAE: Servicio Nacional de Aduana del Ecuador. https://www.aduana.gob.ec/
4. AEADE: Asociación de Empresas Automotrices del Ecuador. http://www.aeade.net/
5. SRI: Matriculación vehicular. http://www.sri.gob.ec/web/guest/matriculacion-vehiculos
6. de Castro, A.F.: Quito: crecimiento y dinámica de una ciudad andina. Revista Geográfica, 121–164 (1989)
7. Singh, M., Rajan, M.A., Shivraj, V.L., Balamuralidhar, P.: Secure MQTT for Internet of Things (IoT). In: 2015 Fifth International Conference on Communication Systems and Network Technologies, pp. 746–751 (2015). https://doi.org/10.1109/CSNT.2015.16
8. Luzuriaga, J.E., Cano, J.C., Calafate, C., Manzoni, P., Perez, M., Boronat, P.: Handling mobility in IoT applications using the MQTT protocol. In: Internet Technologies and Applications (ITA), pp. 245–250. IEEE (2015)
9. Hidalgo. N., Narváez, M., Arteaga, J., Mena, P., Rojas, K.: Plan maestro de movilidad 2009–2025. http://www.flacsoandes.edu.ec/libros/digital/39700.pdf
10. Vanajakshi, L., Ramadurai, G., Anand, A.: Intelligent Transportation systems lecture notes. https://www.thesisscientist.com/docs/StudyNotes/de9b8b1b-3cfc-4d82-8ab0-b4468ff5b3eb
11. ITS-Michigan: Sociedad Inteligente de Transporte de Michigan. http://www.itsmichigan.org/
12. ITS-Rusia: Intelligent Transport Systems of Russia. http://itsrussiaforum.ru/en/
13. Mendez, P.: Red privada virtual como alternativa para el respaldo de información digital en el ilustre municipio de Baños (2017). http://186.3.45.37/bitstream/123456789/7384/1/PIUASIS013-2017.pdf
14. Pigné, Y., Danoy, G., Bouvry, P.: A vehicular mobility model based on real traffic counting data. In: Strang, T., Festag, A., Vinel, A., Mehmood, R., Rico Garcia, C., Röckl, M. (eds.) Nets4Cars/Nets4Trains 2011. LNCS, vol. 6596, pp. 131–142. Springer, Heidelberg (2011). https://doi.org/10.1007/978-3-642-19786-4_12
15. Kamar, E., Horvitz, E., Meek, C.: Mobile opportunistic commerce: mechanisms, architecture, and application. In: Proceedings of the 7th International Joint Conference on Autonomous Agents and Multiagent Systems, vol. 2, pp. 1087–1094. International Foundation for Autonomous Agents and Multiagent Systems, Richland (2008)
16. Ma, H., Zhao, D., Yuan, P.: Opportunities in mobile crowd sensing. IEEE Commun. Mag. **52**, 29–35 (2014). https://doi.org/10.1109/MCOM.2014.6871666
17. Naik, N.: Choice of effective messaging protocols for IoT systems: MQTT, CoAP, AMQP and HTTP. In: 2017 IEEE International Systems Engineering Symposium (ISSE), pp. 1–7 (2017). https://doi.org/10.1109/SysEng.2017.8088251
18. Official Website Arduino: Arduino UNO R3 (2014). https://arduino.cl/arduino-uno/
19. Official Website Raspberry: Raspberry Pi 3. https://www.raspberrypi.org/products/raspberry-pi-3-model-b/

20. CoderProf: gy-gps6mv2 datasheet PDF. http://coderprof.com/PDF_Examples_Free_ Download.php?q=gy-gps6mv2+datasheet
21. Rhydo Technologies (P) Ltd.: SIM 900-RS232 GSM/GPRS Modem User Manual (2011). http://www.rhydolabz.com/documents/gps_gsm/sim900_rs232_gsm_modem_opn.pdf
22. Itead Studio: Raspberry PI GSM Datasheet (2013). ftp://imall.iteadstudio.com/Modules/ IM131224002/DS_IM131224002.pdf
23. Página Oficial EPN: Escuela Politécnica Nacional. https://www.epn.edu.ec/
24. Lim, H.-T., Weckemann, K., Herrscher, D.: Performance study of an in-car switched ethernet network without prioritization. In: Strang, T., Festag, A., Vinel, A., Mehmood, R., Rico Garcia, C., Röckl, M. (eds.) Nets4Cars/Nets4Trains 2011. LNCS, vol. 6596, pp. 165–175. Springer, Heidelberg (2011). https://doi.org/10.1007/978-3-642-19786-4_15
25. OGC® Standards: Sensor Observation Service. https://www.opengeospatial.org/standards/ sos

Air

Performance Evaluation of an AANET in Quito's Control Area

Henry Rivera[1,2], Luis Urquiza-Aguiar[1(✉)] (iD), Xavier Calderón[1], and Ana Zambrano[1]

[1] Departamento de Telecomunicaciones y Redes de Información, Escuela Politécnica Nacional, Ladrón de Guevara E11-253, Quito, Ecuador
{henry.rivera,luis.urquiza,xavier.calderon,ana.zambrano}@epn.edu.ec
[2] Fuerza Aérea Ecuatoriana, Ala de Combate No. 23, Manta, Ecuador
hrivera@fae.mil.ec

Abstract. Nowadays, aircraft can share information through satellite systems and ground infrastructure with limited capacity in terms of air traffic services, operational control, administrative control, as well as connectivity and internet services on board. In particular, ad-hoc networks present some advantages for air navigation connectivity such as distributed operation, infrastructureless (satellite or ground) and low operating costs. This new type of mobile ad-hoc networks is called AANET (Aeronautical Ad-hoc Networks), which have challenges such as very high-speed nodes, large distances between nodes, and limited bandwidth. In this work, the performance evaluation of the classic Ad-Hoc protocols AODV and OLSR, designed for traditional mobile Ad-hoc networks (MANET), is carried out in an AANET using realistic mobility patterns of Quito control area. Our results in the realistic simulation scenario show that OLSR outperforms AODV and it is a feasible candidate for communications between aircraft.

Keywords: AANET · AODV · OLSR · Realistic traces

1 Introduction

The International Civil Aviation Organization (ICAO) have defined along the years several communication capabilities that support the aeronautical activity. Some of these services are Air Traffic Services Communication (ATSC), Aeronautical Operation Control (AOC), Aeronautical Administrative Control (Aeronautical Administrative Control AAC), Aeronautical Passenger Communication (APC). However, they have limitations such as low bandwidth, complex and

The authors gratefully acknowledge the financial support provided by the Escuela Politécnica Nacional, for the development of the project PIJ-15-20 "E-iRoads: Ecuador - Inteligent Roads. Un Sistema inteligente para la gestión de tráfico en las periferias de grandes ciudades (Caso de Estudio: Quito)". H. Rivera and L. Urquiza contributed equally to this paper.

B. Hilt et al. (Eds.): Nets4Cars/Nets4Trains/Nets4Aircraft 2019, LNCS 11461, pp. 73–85, 2019.
https://doi.org/10.1007/978-3-030-25529-9_7

expensive infrastructure onboard or land [20], high costs to provide telephony and Internet services, and considerable delays [3]. The reason for this problem is the limited link's capacity between an aircraft and a land station or between two aircraft, mostly used for onboard sensors data and crew communications. Therefore, ad-hoc networks would have some advantages for air navigation connectivity such as distributed operation, no need of infrastructure (satellite or ground), extended coverage range thanks to their multi-hop nature and low operating costs [11]. In particular, some studies have focused their attention in a new kind of ad-hoc networks formed by aircraft, named Aeronautical Ad-hoc Networks (AANETs) [5,15], which is a special case of Fly Ad-hoc Network; nonetheless FANETs have been associated more directly with ad-hoc networks formed by UAVs (Unmanned Air Vehicles). They have specific challenges such as very high-speed nodes, large distances between nodes, and connectivity depending on the access medium technology [8]. Nonetheless, AANETs could make safer trips by providing real-time awareness of nearby aircraft [6].

AANETs, like other ad-hoc networks, have been studied through analytic models and mostly by using network and movement simulators. However, the lack of real movement traces or realistic synthetic traces readable by network simulators, have caused that there are few studies on the performance of ad-hoc routing protocols with reliable mobility patterns while others use simple models as Random Way Point or similar with adequate parameters. For instance, in [6] the isolation probability of an aircraft is computed at different altitudes and using VHF links. Medina et. al. in [7] and [8] analyze the feasibility of an AANET under a topological point of view and using a simple greedy algorithm over European airspace and the North Atlantic Corridor; their results show that it is possible to reach high connectivity and packet delivery ratio. In [16] a relaying protocol with TDMA is proposed to mitigate the weakness of HF channels, the protocol was tested using North Pacific Ocean routes with a random generation time of aircraft. Besse et. al. [2] show the feasibility and good performance of an AANET by using realistic traces from air control traffic of France, pre-computed shortest paths with OPNET simulator and considering W-CDMA for uplinks and DVB-S2 for downlinks. Vey et. al. [20] propose an AANET aircraft to aircraft to ground stations, with a bandwidth of 20 MHz in the 2 GHz band and using Direct Sequence CDMA (DS-CDMA) for North Atlantic and French airspaces. As in [2], authors of [20] use predefined routes but a proprietary simulator. Authors of [15] uses their own simulator to show the better performance of their proposed routing protocol against DSR for AANETs, however, random movement generation was employed. Vey et.al. [19] perform a comparative analysis of AODV, DYMO, and BATMAN protocols with historical repository trajectories aircraft over North Atlantic corridor using their MAC proposal named RPCDMA (Random Packet CDMA); their results shows that AODV outperforms the other protocols. Other works, such as [21] uses unrealistic movement of aircraft to evaluate the performance of routing protocols. Most of the studies of ad-hoc routing protocols in FANETs have been done considering UAVs. Good reviews of their performance in UAVs, advantage, and limitations can be found in [9] and [14].

On the contrary of the aforementioned works, this paper presents the performance evaluation of two classic ad-hoc protocols designed for traditional mobile networks such as AODV and OLSR in aeronautical networks in the relatively small air control area of Quito, Ecuador. More precisely, the contribution of this work is twofold:

1. Our performance evaluation is carried out with realistic mobility patterns in three dimensions.
2. We use the OFDM physical with a channel spacing of 5 MHz and MAC layer of the IEEE 802.11 standard. Our intention is to test the performance of the AANET with cheap and non-licensed technology.

The rest of this paper is organized as follows: Sect. 2 describes how we generated synthetic, realistic aircraft' mobility traces to incorporate them to NS-3 simulator. After that, Sect. 3 presents the results obtained of comparing AODV against OLSR by varying flight's factors. Finally, Sect. 4 draws some conclusions and future work.

2   Materials and Methods

In this section, we explain how we generate realistic aircraft traces for the control area of Quito and the integration with NS-3 network simulator.

2.1   Generation of Flight Mobility Traces

Air mobility is highly dynamic, so it requires three-dimensional models, however, most of the models available in the NS-3 simulator are designed for two dimensions and have a predetermined structure of initial positioning such as grid, rectangle or disk in a random way. Since aircraft are objects moving over the air, flights' simulation must follow physics laws and the trajectories cannot be random. More specifically, an aircraft's position at a given point depends on the previous position and a velocity vector. Therefore a good flight simulator requires memory to generate realistic flight traces.

In this work, we use realistic mobility traces based on the artificial recreation of aircraft flights generated by a trail-version of STK with Aviator Add-on [1]. STK is a three-dimensional simulator which satisfies a large number of parameters and physical variables, including the man factor (e.g. for planning the flight maneuver). More specifically, Aviator allows us to simulate flight considering parameters such as type of aircraft, characteristics of airstrips, the maneuver of take-off and landing, bearing and range of destination and en-route properties (e.g. altitude, cruising speed). We create four simulation cases corresponding to four parameters of a flight that present typical variations. These evaluated parameters are altitude of flight, aircraft speed, wind direction, and aircraft performance. The last parameter depends on the type of aircraft used in the flight. Table 1 summarizes the information of the first three parameters and Table 2 include the types of aircraft used in the simulations.

Table 1. Simulation scenarios

Scenarios	Parameters	Value
1	Altitude	**15000 ft** 25000 ft 35000 ft
2	Aircraft's speed*	Min. air speed 84.1112 nm/hr **Max. performance air speed 314.74 nm/hr** Max. endurance air speed 171.417 nm/hr
3	Wind direction	0°, **30 nm/hr** 90°, 30 nm/hr 180°, 30 nm/hr

nm/hr: Nautical miles/hour
* These values are typical for a conventional aircraft.

Table 2. Air traffic generated with STK simulator

No.	Origin	Dest.	Code of flight		Performance		
					One	Two	Three
1	Quito	Guayaquil	SEQM	SEGU	Basic airliner	Basic general aviation	Basic business jet
2	Cuenca	Quito	SECU	SEQM	Basic airliner	Basic business jet	Basic turbo-propeller
3	Esmeraldas	Quito	SETN	SEQM	Basic airliner	Basic general aviation	Basic turbo-propeller
4	Shell	Manta	SESM	SEMT	Basic turbo-propeller	Basic helicopter	Basic airliner
5	Latacunga	Manta	SELT	SEMT	Basic military transport	Basic fighter	Basic airliner
6	Manta	Quito	SEMT	SEQM	Basic general aviation	Basic business jet	Basic military transport
7	Quevedo	Quito	SEQE	SEQM	Basic helicopter	Basic turbo-propeller	Basic fighter
8	Salinas	Quito	SESA	SEQM	Basic fighter	Basic airliner	Basic military transport
9	Santa Rosa	Quito	SERO	SEQM	Basic military transport	Basic helicopter	Basic airliner
10	Guayaquil	Macas	SEGU	SEMC	Basic general aviation	Basic military transport	Basic helicopter

For each parameter, we consider three different values that are close to the reality of Ecuadorian domestic flights. For each parameter value, we generate simulation traces from two to ten simultaneous flights in order to evaluate their influence in the AANET's performance in NS-3. As we stated, in this paper, the aircraft's performance is modeled by using different types of aircraft.

Bold values in Table 1 are used by default in the simulations. Additionally, Table 2 shows the flights simulated for air control area of Quito with three different performances (i.e. types of aircraft). For the comparisons performed in the next section, performance 1 is used by default. Figure 1 provides a general view of the ten flights generated with STK simulator. It is worth to note that Aviator will change phases and procedures of the flights according to the parameter value that we have set. More important, Aviator includes the geographical features of the airports' location. This means that take-off and landing procedures are very close to reality because they adapt to the particularity of the airports such as near obstacles (mountains) and runway's length.

Finally, the traces of the flight simulation performed with STK are obtained through the reports option. For each aircraft, the position and velocity have to be saved in ECEF coordinates. With this configuration, STK will generate a text file with time, position in x, y and z coordinates and the speed of aircraft for every second of the simulation time.

Fig. 1. 3D plot of the 10 flight traces generated with STK for Quito's air control area.

2.2   Setting up AANET Scenarios in NS-3

For a successful simulation of an AANET in NS-3, the correct execution of the steps depicted in Fig. 2 should be done. The key step is to read the report generated by STK to proper temporally store time, position and speed of each aircraft (step 2 of Fig. 2). With this information, the waypoint mobility model has to be used to provide movement to the created nodes (step 3). The remaining steps are identical to any ad-hoc simulation of NS-3 and include the creation of devices (to configure the routing protocols), the installation of applications to generate and receive data traffic and monitor add-on to generate reports.

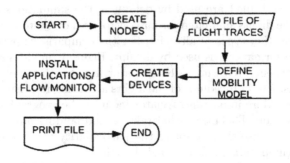

Fig. 2. Flow chart to code an AANET simulation with realistic traces

Regarding the values of parameters configured in the simulation, we employ the standard IEEE 802.11 at the physical and MAC layer. More precisely, we use the OFDM at 5 GHz physical layer with "quarter-clocked" operation using 5 MHz channel spacing with data communication capabilities of 1.5, 2.25, 3, 4.5, 6, 9, 12, and 13.5 Mb/s [4]. As reference IEEE 802.11p uses OFDM with "half-clocked" using bandwidth of 10 MHz. The main idea behind our selection is to get more robust communication channels. Aircraft were set with a power transmission of 40 dBm, similar to used in real data links equipment for aviation [13] and antenna gain of 3dBi. In addition, we use Friis propagation loss model. Other parameters, including configurations of AODV and OLSR, were set by default. Table 3 summarizes the specific values configured in the simulation.

Table 3. Simulation settings.

Parameter	Value
Physical layer	IEEE 802.11 OFDM
Channel BW	5 MHz
MAC specification	IEEE 802.11
Transmission power	40 dbm
Antenna gain	3 dbi
Mobility generator	Aviator, STK
Path loss model	Friis
Bandwidth	3 Mbps
Routing protocol	AODV, OLSR

3   Simulation Results

In this section, we show the results from comparing AODV against OLSR in the AANET of the air control area of Quito. AODV [10] is a reactive protocol that uses the Bellman-Ford distance vector algorithm which was adapted to work in a mobile environment. It determines an end-to-end route to a destination only when a source node wants to send a packet. Routes are maintained as long as they are needed by the source while there is connectivity between nodes in the path. Therefore, protocol signaling messages are only used when traffic needs to be sent. On the other hand, OLSR [12] is a proactive link-state routing protocol, which uses hello messages to detect to 2-hops neighbors and select multipoint relays (MPRs). MPRs forward and select the proper route from any source to any desired destination node. MPRs periodically broadcast topology control (TC) messages to maintain updated the state of the mobile ad hoc network. As proactive protocol, in OLSR, routes to all destinations within the network are known before use, therefore transmission delay is generally shorter than in reactive ones. In addition, if the topology does not change very fast then the overhead should not be much greater than in a reactive protocol.

To obtain our results, we have ranged the number of aircraft in the air from 2 to 10 in steps of 2 by adding new flights in the order generated in Table 2. In all simulations, we generate traffic UDP at 1 kbps (e.g. monitoring traffic) from aircraft number 1 to aircraft number 2. Aircraft 1 serves the route Quito-Guayaquil, which is the most popular domestic flight of Ecuador due to it connects the two biggest cities in the country. Aircraft number 2, which receives the UDP traffic, departures from Cuenca (the third biggest city) to Guayaquil. In the following, the results are presented in terms of Packet loss ratio and average end-to-end delay. We ran ten simulations changing the simulation seed for each scenario with a (i.e., combination number of nodes and parameter). So, in total, we ran 600 simulations to obtain the results of this section.

3.1   Altitude

We tested three values of altitude of the flight (15000, 25000 and 35000 ft) with the default parameters of Table 1 (i.e. bold values). This parameter affects the processes of departure and landing because as the altitude increases the time spent in both maneuvers increase as well. Figure 3 shows that the altitude of a flight does not affect the performance of any of both protocols. Only a slight difference in the delay of AODV is observed when then aircraft are in the air (see Fig. 3a). Regarding, the difference between AODV and OLSR, results indicate that OLSR always performs better or, in the worse case, equal to AODV.

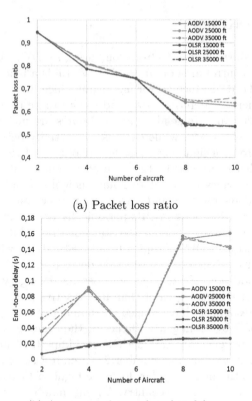

(a) Packet loss ratio

(b) Average end-to-end packet delay.

Fig. 3. Performance comparison between AODV and OLSR at different flight altitudes.

3.2   Wind Direction

Wind is a paramount factor that affects the maneuverability of an aircraft. To this analysis we use a constant speed of 30 nm/hr but three different directions. Wind at 0° is a headwind, the most favourable to fly an aircraft. Crosswind 90° and tailwind (180°) are more challenging to navigate aircraft, especially the latter. Again, OLSR outperforms in both metrics to AODV, as can be seen in Fig. 4. The headwind leads to higher Packet loss ratio in OLSR than with other wind directions, while with AODV this is true until 6 nodes. The packets' delay is not affected by the wind direction in the case of OLSR. In AODV, the delay is higher than in other two cases when there are six or more aircraft. A reason for higher losses and delay with headwind could be that it helps to a easy flight, so nodes can go faster than in the other cases to destinations.

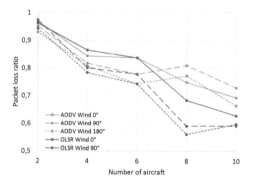

(a) Packet loss ratio

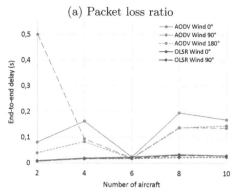

(b) Average end-to-end packet delay.

Fig. 4. Performance comparison between AODV and OLSR at wind direction.

3.3 Speed of Aircraft

Cruising speed used by aircraft in a flight could affect the performance of routing protocols because high speeds will make network topology also change very fast, so routing protocols would use outdated information for their routing decisions. Figure 5 confirms this hypothesis, as the speed of aircraft increases, the performance of both routing protocols decrease. This is the Packet loss ratio increases (Fig. 5a) and the average delay (Fig. 5b).

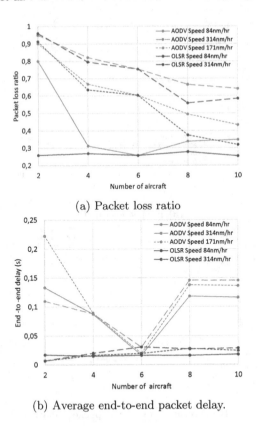

(a) Packet loss ratio

(b) Average end-to-end packet delay.

Fig. 5. Performance comparison between AODV and OLSR at different aircraft' speed

3.4   Performance of Aircraft

The objective of this test is to find out if the types of aircraft used to do the ten flights can affect the performance of routing protocols. As we have stated in Sect. 2.1, "performance one" in Table 2 is the typical types of aircraft serving the ten routes and "performance three" are the least common. Performance two and three include the use of helicopters and more military transport than in performance one. We are aware that it is unlikely that all flights be served by aircraft of performance two or three at the same time. Nonetheless, our intention is to see how large can be the performance gap of the routing protocols in such uncommon situations.

Our results, depicted in Fig. 6 indicate that performance one is the most favorable types of aircraft for OLSR in terms of packet losses. The high average delay, in this case, is due to the fact that more packets (from farther distances) reach the destination. The third configuration of aircraft is the worse scenario for OLSR in terms of losses and delay. In the case of AODV, the types of aircraft used in "performance two" get the best marks in both losses and delay. We highlight the fact that with this configuration AODV matches the Packet loss ratio

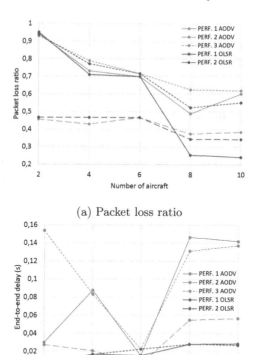

(a) Packet loss ratio

(b) Average end-to-end packet delay.

Fig. 6. Performance metrics results.

obtained by OLSR but with a higher delay than OLSR. Moreover, "performance three" is also the worst-case scenario for AODV and its performance is close to OLSR's results Packet loss ratio.

3.5   Comparative Analysis

In all the factors analyzed, OLSR shows a better performance than AODV in both the Packet loss ratio and the average end-to-end delay. In addition, for all studied factors (i.e. altitude, wind direction, aircraft's speed and performance) there the results depends of the number of nodes. More precisely, as the number of nodes increases, the packet losses rate decreases and the average delay increases. The best results for both protocols among all the test, were obtained when aircraft were to set to a cruising speed of 84 nm/hr.

   The better behavior of OLSR compared to AODV is due to characteristics of aerial scenario. Flights follow a predefined path with few changes of directions. This helps OLSR to have updated routing tables in all most of the time. It is worth to note that the behavior of AODV protocol with 6 nodes is due to the fact that nodes 5 and 6 serve routes that remain in the center of the simulated area, therefore they increase the connectivity in the network. When more nodes are added to the simulation, AODV creates long routes and they break frequently.

4 Conclusions and Future Work

We have tested two classic ad-hoc routing protocols in a relative small AANET scenario that corresponds to the control area of Quito. To obtain reliable results we have used realistic, synthetic movement traces generated by STK simulator with NS-3 simulator. The traces considered important flight factors like type of aircraft, cruising speed, altitude, and wind direction. Moreover, we provide an idea of the base behavior of routing protocols by using a simple physical and MAC layer with realistic settings.

Our results indicate that proactive protocols like OLSR outperforms reactive approaches such as AODV because of the predictive movement of aircraft. Our study also shows that some parameters of a flight like cruising speed and wind direction would have a significant impact on the routing performance.

As future work, we are planning to adapt and test geographical routing protocols like [17,18] in AANET scenarios because they consider speed and direction of nodes in their routing decisions.

References

1. AGI, Inc.: System Tool Kit (STK) (2019). https://www.agi.com/products/engineering-tools
2. Besse, F., Garcia, F., Pirovano, A., Radzik, J.: 28th AIAA International Communications Satellite Systems Conference (ICSSC 2010). American Institute of Aeronautics and Astronautics, August (2010). https://doi.org/10.2514/6.2010-8795
3. Hoffmann, F.: Routing and internet gateway selection in aeronautical ad hoc networks (2015)
4. IEEE: IEEE Standard for Information technology-telecommunications and information exchange between systems Local and metropolitan area networks-Specific requirements Part 11: Wireless LAN Medium Access Control (MAC) and Physical Layer (PHY) Specifications (2012). https://doi.org/10.1109/IEEESTD.2012.6178212
5. Karras, K., Kyritsis, T., Amirfeiz, M., Baiotti, S.: Aeronautical mobile ad hoc networks. In: 2008 14th European Wireless Conference, June, pp. 1–6. IEEE (2008). https://doi.org/10.1109/EW.2008.4623845
6. Li, H., Yang, B., Chen, C., Guan, X.: Connectivity of aeronautical ad hoc networks. In: 2010 IEEE Globecom Workshops, December, pp. 1788–1792 (2010). https://doi.org/10.1109/GLOCOMW.2010.5700249
7. Medina, D., Hoffmann, F., Ayaz, S., Rokitansky, C.H.: Feasibility of an aeronautical mobile ad hoc network over the North Atlantic corridor. In: 2008 5th Annual IEEE Communications Society Conference on Sensor, Mesh and Ad Hoc Communications and Networks, June, pp. 109–116. IEEE (2008). https://doi.org/10.1109/SAHCN.2008.23

8. Medina, D., Hoffmann, F., Ayaz, S., Rokitansky, C.H.: Topology characterization of high density airspace aeronautical ad hoc networks. In: 2008 5th IEEE International Conference on Mobile Ad Hoc and Sensor Systems, September, pp. 295–304. IEEE (2008). https://doi.org/10.1109/MAHSS.2008.4660016

9. Oubbati, O.S., Lakas, A., Zhou, F., Güneş, M., Yagoubi, M.B.: A survey on position-based routing protocols for Flying Ad hoc Networks (FANETs). Veh. Commun. **10**, 29–56 (2017). https://doi.org/10.1016/J.VEHCOM.2017.10.003

10. Perkins, C., Belding-Royer, E., Das, S.: Request For Comments: 3561 Ad hoc On-Demand Distance Vector (AODV) Routing. Internet Engineering Task Force - Network Working Group, pp. 1–13 (2003)

11. Perkins, C.E., et al.: Ad Hoc Networking, vol. 1. Addison-Wesley, Reading (2001)

12. Project Hipercom, I.: Request For Comments: 3626 Optimized Link State Routing Protocol (OLSR). Internet Engineering Task Force - Network Working Group, pp. 1–75 (2003)

13. Rohde & Schwarz: M3AR Software Defined Radios VHF/UHF transceiver family for airborne communications (2009)

14. Sahingoz, O.K.: Networking models in flying ad-hoc networks (FANETs): concepts and challenges. J. Intell. Robot. Syst. **74**(1), 513–527 (2014). https://doi.org/10.1007/s10846-013-9959-7

15. Sakhaee, E., Jamalipour, A., Kato, N.: Aeronautical ad hoc networks. In: 2006 IEEE Wireless Communications and Networking Conference. WCNC 2006, pp. 246–251. IEEE (2006). https://doi.org/10.1109/WCNC.2006.1683472

16. Tu, H.D., Shimamoto, S.: A proposal of relaying data in aeronautical communication for oceanic flight routes employing mobile ad-hoc network. In: 2009 First Asian Conference on Intelligent Information and Database Systems, April, pp. 436–441. IEEE (2009). https://doi.org/10.1109/ACIIDS.2009.91

17. Urquiza-Aguiar, L., Igartua, M., Tripp-Barba, C., Calderón-Hinojosa, X.: 2hGAR: 2-hops geographical anycast routing protocol for vehicle-to-infrastructure communications. In: MobiWac 2017 - Proceedings of the 15th ACM International Symposium on Mobility Management and Wireless Access, Co-located with MSWiM 2017 (2017). https://doi.org/10.1145/3132062.3132076

18. Urquiza-Aguiar, L., Tripp-Barba, C., Aguilar Igartua, M.: A geographical heuristic routing protocol for VANETs. Sensors **16**(10), 1567 (2016). https://doi.org/10.3390/s16101567

19. Vey, Q., Pirovano, A., Radzik, J.: Performance analysis of routing algorithms in AANET with realistic access layer. In: Mendizabal, J., et al. (eds.) Nets4Cars/Nets4Trains/Nets4Aircraft 2016. LNCS, vol. 9669, pp. 175–186. Springer, Cham (2016). https://doi.org/10.1007/978-3-319-38921-9_18

20. Vey, Q., Pirovano, A., Radzik, F., Garcia, F.: Aeronautical ad hoc network for civil aviation. In: Sikora, A., Berbineau, M., Vinel, A., Jonsson, M., Pirovano, A., Aguado, M. (eds.) Nets4Cars/Nets4Trains/Nets4Aircraft 2014. LNCS, vol. 8435, pp. 81–93. Springer, Cham (2014). https://doi.org/10.1007/978-3-319-06644-8_8

21. Zhou, Q., Gu, W., Li, J., Sun, Q., Yang, F.: A topology aware routing protocol based ADS-B system for aeronautical ad hoc networks. In: 2012 8th International Conference on Wireless Communications, Networking and Mobile Computing, pp. 1–4. IEEE (2012). https://doi.org/10.1109/WiCOM.2012.6478379

GreenSword: Green Space Cleaning Using an Autonomous Swarm of Heterogeneous Drones - First Retex

Raphaël Anquetil[2], Vincent Autefage[1], Serge Chaumette[2(✉)], and Sébastien Pouteau[2]

[1] Univ. Bordeaux, 33400 Talence, France
[2] Univ. Bordeaux, CNRS, Bordeaux INP, LaBRI, UMR5800, 33400 Talence, France
serge.chaumette@labri.fr
http://www.labri.fr/

Abstract. Since a few years, the number of real world applications that use drones keeps on increasing. It has also been demonstrated that swarms of heterogeneous drones can offer more features and thus support more services than single drones. While working on this paradigm, we have developed an application that makes it possible to clean a green space, using an autonomous swarm of heterogeneous drones (aerial and terrestrial). This application is called GreenSword. We describe the underlying scientific challenges of this system, our current implementation and give the retex we gained from initial experiments.

Keywords: GreenSword · Green space cleaning · Drones · Robots · Swarms · Resilience · Autonomous systems

1 Introduction

1.1 Context

Today, drones are used in an increasing number of situations even though these very often remain experimental, mainly because of regulation issues. Additionally, the ability to combine a set of possibly heterogeneous drones (ground, air, surface, submarine), thus building heterogeneous swarms, raises interest in both the industry and the academy.

We have been working on swarms of drones since 2009 [10], and based on our expertise, we claim that a swarm of drones is more efficient than individual systems [8]. The drawback in that in such configurations, failure is the nominal mode of operation [9] because of the number of systems that are involved. Therefore, to achieve a given mission, one as to take this issue into consideration, and must thus carefully redesign each application, which is quite different from what it would be in a stable system where failure would be the exception.

B. Hilt et al. (Eds.): Nets4Cars/Nets4Trains/Nets4Aircraft 2019, LNCS 11461, pp. 86–97, 2019.
https://doi.org/10.1007/978-3-030-25529-9_8

Among the other major issues of swarming is the location of a given resource (camera, chemical nose, etc...) in the swarm. This is what we addressed in one of the projects of our road-map; GreenSword, the *cleaning scenario*, was born during this work, as a significant experimentation use case.

1.2 The Green Space Cleaning Project

As explained above, this project was initially an experimentation target for our theoretical research. It has quickly raised interest, especially among our industry partners and among funding bodies. Indeed, the presence of waste in our environment is something recurrent and very difficult to deal with. Today, the solutions rely on people employed to carry out this cleaning almost manually. It is a laborious task that requires a lot of time and investment and is not very rewarding. This clearly falls into the 3D (*Dull, Dangerous, Dirty* [11]) paradigm where drones can help. Our approach, that solves the problem using advance technology, is thus appealing.

In this paper, we propose a solution (which is one of the output of our research experiments) that makes it possible to free humans from this dull and possibly dirty task. This solution is based on the use of ground drones (called rovers in what follows) and of aerial drones (simply called drones).

2 From an Initial Theoretical Issue to a Real World Application

2.1 Initial Challenge: Locating a Resource in a Heterogeneous Swarm

The theoretical issue that we have been addressing in the fundamental work that gave birth to the greenspace cleaning scenario is how to find a given resource in a highly unstable mobile network. This is called *service discovery*.

Service discovery is the way for an entity or node (*i.e.* a client) to locate a capability (*i.e.* a service) which is available on another node (*i.e.* a provider) within the network. Despite the existence of many service discovery mechanisms, several problems are still open [4,19]:

- *Service usage* (*i.e.* the way to access a service once it has been discovered) is not addressed in most existing solutions.
- *Service selection* which is required when a given service is hosted by several different nodes is also often ignored.
- The *performance* of MANet applications is closely dependent on the mobility of the nodes of the network [7,12]. This is due to the fact that mobility has a strong impact on connectivity patterns [18]. A service discovery mechanism should thus be able to adapt its behavior to this parameter. This is hardly ever considered.

- *Resilience*: the volatility of the network must be dealt with to support what we call degraded mode of operation (faulty vehicle, lost communication, etc...). It must be possible for nodes (providers or clients) to join or to leave the network at any time without jeopardizing the mission currently run by the swarm.
- *Autonomy*: to ensure degraded mode of operation (see above), each node of the swarm should be totally autonomous and take its own decisions. In other words, there can be no supervisor, *i.e.*no entity should play a central role.

These limitations of the approaches described in the literature encouraged us to develop our own system called AMiRALE [4,5] (*Asynchronous Missions Relay for Autonomous and Lively Entities*) which focuses on the actions induced by services rather than by their location in the network. The system thus becomes resource location independent. By doing so, AMiRALE enables a swarm of mobile nodes to perform tasks collaboratively, offering solutions to most (if not all) of the problems listed above.

The systems that we address operate on an underlying model which is reactive. It means that a certain set of events (*e.g.* exceeding temperature threshold, making a suspicious movement, etc.) require a reaction of the swarm (*e.g.* making some additional measurement, triggering an alarm, etc.). A *mission* is the set of information that describes such an action to be performed by the swarm. A *sensor node* is a node that is able to detect an event (through its physical hardware sensors) and to create the corresponding mission. A *solver node* is a node that is able to achieve the specific actions required by the mission. Finally, a *forwarder node* is a node which forwards a mission to the members of the swarm. A swarm must by nature be able to manage several types of missions, and each node can thus have several roles. Moreover, a sensor node for a specific mission type is not always a solver for this same type (because of energy consumption, space or weight limitations, etc.). Each node has its own clock, its own memory (which stores, among others, the mission related information) and a unique identifier. At a regular time interval, nodes share some parts of their database with their currently available neighbors (*i.e.* neighbors with which they can communicate at the considered instant) and update the status of the missions they are aware of, based on the information they receive from other nodes. There is no synchronization between the nodes, all operations are made locally and communications are performed using broadcasts only. This makes it possible to support resilience (when either nodes or messages are lost). Since several decisions and optimizations are by nature application dependent (*e.g.* creating a new mission for an event which has already been circulated, not sharing a mission because it has been shared enough for a certain period of time, etc.), AMiRALE includes several user definable functions called *filters* that can be used to improve the behavior of the distributed system for the target scenario.

2.2 Scenario: Green Space Cleaning

As explained above, the greenspace cleaning scenario was initially conceived solely for illustration purpose. It has evolved a great deal since then and has raised interest in the industry and in some public institutions.

The action takes place in an environment in which wastes are randomly spread. The greenspace cleaning system (which was initially called ParCS [3] and which is now called GreenSword) offers a solution to achieve a selective collection of wastes by using an autonomous swarm of drones and rovers. These vehicles are self-organized. Each rover is specialized, which means that it can only collect a specific type of garbage (*e.g.* paper, glass, compost, plastic).

The green space (and the position of the wastes) is obviously not known in advance and when the system is put into operation, a certain amount of time will be allocated to the recognition of the site. While flying drones will fly over in search of wastes that they can detect with their cameras, rovers will move in the environment determining whether they can pick up wastes around them.

Regarding the flying drones, as soon as one has identified a waste, it informs any rover (or drone) passing nearby of the presence of the waste and of its position. If a rover that receives this information is not performing another assigned task (actually picking up another waste) and is specialized in this given waste type, it will move to the indicated location and pick up the waste. If the rover cannot pickup this kind of waste, it just passes the information to any other rover or drone that passes nearby. Drones act as unspecialized rovers, *i.e* as rovers that cannot pick up wastes. They just circulate information around.

When a rover considers that it has enough waste on board, it moves to a landfill area defined before the operation is launched, where it dumps the wastes it has collected. Since rovers and drones have limited autonomy, a charging station is also set up.

In this scenario, AMiRALE is used as follows. The mission type e represents a type of garbage. A robot or drone which is able to detect a garbage of type e is a *sensor* for garbage type e. A robot which can clean a garbage of type e is a *solver* for garbage type e. User definable *filters* provided by AMiRALE are configured to optimize the garbage selection process and the message broadcast mechanisms.

3 Real World Implementation

In the initial demonstrations we have focused our efforts on the rovers, which must be able to move around, to locate themselves and to avoid obstacles in an autonomous manner.

3.1 Making Localization of the Rovers Autonomous

One of the major advantages for using the GreenSword cleaning system is the autonomy of the drones and of the rovers once they are released in the field.

To achieve this autonomy, in addition to using the AMiRALE based algorithm described above, they must be able to move around autonomously. This is not a real issue for drones which fly in a free space but it is one for the rovers.

To accomplish this task, we had to make the most out of the embedded sensors, which sometimes proved to be insufficient. We first tried to use the embedded camera to capture what is around to feed SLAM (Simultaneous Localization and Mapping) [2]. SLAM consists in using the images provided by a camera to build or improve a map of the environment of the rover, while simultaneously locating it within this map. Algorithms describing this method and implementations already exist [2,6]. The problem is that for this technique to be effective, the input data must be of good quality. But the reality is far from perfect and we very often encounter problems of brightness (either the images are too dark, or too bright) in which case we do not manage to process the information in a manner that would allow the rover to estimate its location.

Another problem is performance. The autopilot system provided by the rover did not work properly, so we had to resort to an alternative. For cost reasons, we have decided on using a Raspberry Pi 3 which unfortunately does not offer the necessary computing power. Even if we had a good output from our camera, the number of frames per second we can acquire and the processing time of these frames would make the use of SLAM inefficient. The embedded lidar and ultrasonic sensors do not either provide a usable view of the environment because they are fixed and therefore only locate things around or in front of them on one single plane. However, they will be very useful to avoid obstacles.

Finally, the rovers that we use do not provide reliable odometry [13,14,20]. A good odometry would have allowed to determine the precise distance covered by the rover and this would have supported the localization process.

All these elements together made the movements of the rovers difficult to deal with and another solution had to be implemented.

In the context of this first prototype, we therefore proposed to create landmarks in the environment. For this purpose, it was decided to use ArUco markers (Fig. 1). They are described in [15] as follows:

An ArUco marker is a synthetic square marker composed by a wide black border and an inner binary matrix which determines its identifier (id). The black border facilitates its fast detection in the image and the binary codification allows its identification and the application of error detection and correction techniques. The marker size determines the size of the internal matrix. For instance a marker size of 4 × 4 is composed of 16 bits.

To use these markers, an initialization phase is required where the position of the tags must be set on a virtual map. A rover then knows, when it identifies a tag on the ground, where it is by referring to this map. This solution works very well but it still has some drawbacks. We have to instrument the area where we intend to operate with tags, which can be an issue especially when we have a very large area. Moreover, if one or more tags disappear, the rovers can quickly get lost.

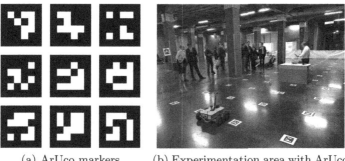

(a) ArUco markers   (b) Experimentation area with ArUco markers

Fig. 1. Localization based on ArUco markers in a demonstration area

This solution was developed using ROS [17], which is a specialized software development platform for robots. ROS provides a stack of blocks that makes it possible to retrieve information from the rover, process it and define its behavior accordingly.

3.2 Obstacle Avoidance

Another central issue related to the autonomy of the rovers is their ability to manage their movements in the environment. They must identify the obstacles that are around them and of course avoid them. To achieve this goal, we use a lidar placed on top of the rover and an ultrasonic sensor located on the front and at a slightly lower height than the lidar. The lidar retrieves information in all directions while the ultrasonic sensor retrieves information only from the front of the rover and at a shorter distance. By combining these two sources of information, robust obstacle avoidance can be achieved.

To take advantage of the lidar, we have defined detection zones that we use to decide on the behaviour of the rover. We have decided on 7 different areas (see Fig. 2): front left, front right, left, right, backleft, backright and back. Depending on whether something is detected in a given area, an obstacle is considered present or not in this area. Typically, if the rover detects something in the front left or left area, it will turn right. Since the lidar is not centered on the rover and since the rover itself has a rectangular shape, each zone is given a different distance detection threshold. This threshold has been measured in real life. This calibration step was particularly important for the detection of obstacles very close to the wheels: if something is detected from too far away, the rover will turn too early, and conversely if something is detected when too close, the rover will either hit the obstacle or turn too late and rub it.

Till now, we have only tested our algorithm indoor in a relatively narrow space. Still, the results of these tests allow us to foresee a good operational efficiency of our approach when we move to an external environment.

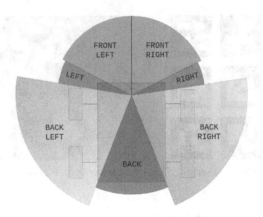

Fig. 2. Lidar detection zones

4   Simulation: A Mandatory Step Between Theory and Practice

We created a 3D simulation to provide a representation of what the project will look like once completed. To do this, we used a game engine called Unity [16]. Unity provides a large number of features and tools that make it possible to produce prototypes very quickly. The goal was to put a fleet of drones and rovers in a situation, to make them communicate and interact with each other in a green space environment.

The simulation works as follows. We have built a map divided into a finite number of areas on which drones and rovers are placed. When the simulation is launched, the rovers move arbitrarily on this map while the drones move at varying altitudes in an attempt to detect wastes (Fig. 3). If a drone detects a waste, it transmits the information to any drone or rover that passes nearby. It should be noted that each rover is intended to collect one single type of waste. It must thus be able to work out when approaching a target whether it is a waste that it can handle or not.

Of course, it is a question of creating the same constraints as in reality to test and show how our system/algorithms behave in the real life. This is why obstacles (especially trees) have been scattered over the entire map and should be avoided without their position being known in advance. In addition, we have implemented an algorithm to compensate for a possible failure of one of the robots, that will distribute the abandoned areas equally.

(a) A rover heading towards a waste

(b) The drones scanning the area

Fig. 3. Simulation of the GreenSword project using Unity

5 Initial Prototype

As a result of all the above considerations, we have built a first prototype based on hardware acquired in the framework of a previous projects. These include several drones and rovers (Fig. 4).

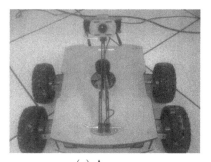 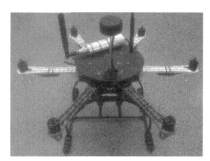

(a) A rover

(b) A drone

Fig. 4. Initial experimental platforms

The rovers (see Fig. 4a) are based on a piwhawk [1] autopilot. Each embeds a camera, a lidar, distance sensors plus of course all the motion mechanics and electronics. The drones (see Fig. 4b) are basically build around the same configuration.

6 First Experimentations and Initial Retex

We have run two real life experimentations till now.

6.1   First Experimentation in Our Laboratory

For the first experimentation, the allocated space was approximately $50\,\mathrm{m}^2$ with 2/3 of this area secured with nets so that drones could fly safely. We encountered a number of issues. Some were related to the physical experimentation area: we had to secure it so as to be able to fly drones. Since this was a private demonstration in our laboratory, this was not a too constraining concern, but we also had to secure the room from damages that could come from the drones in case of a crash. Once done (see Fig. 5), we began experimenting.

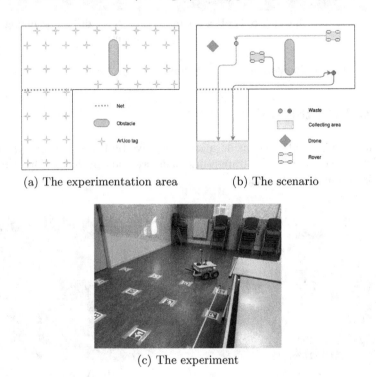

(a) The experimentation area   (b) The scenario

(c) The experiment

Fig. 5. First experimentation in our laboratory

Experimenting indoor is always a problem because we have to deal with a GPS denied environment. Therefore as described Sect. 3.1, we initially based our work on Simultaneous Location & Mapping (SLAM) using the embedded camera. It quickly appeared that the bad lighting of the room and the poor quality of the camera made it almost impossible to work. Therefore we decided on using QRcode like tags (ArUco tags, see Sect. 3.1) stuck on the ground and regularly spaced. This made it possible to solve this issue, but, of course, this is not a long term solution because in the real life it will not be possible to instrument the experimentation area. Additionally, for this first run we did not have time to include odometry in the rovers. The movements of the rovers were thus very stutter and quite slow.

6.2   Second Experiment in a Larger Venue

The second experimentation was run with much more space, in a location called H14 in Bordeaux (Fig. 6). We had $100\,m^2$, with half of this surface secured to make it possible to fly drones. Safety of the public was especially important because we had around 1500 visitors (in two days) who came to see the demonstration and to interact with the team.

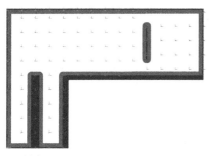
(a) The experimentation area

(b) Real life experimentation in H14

Fig. 6. Second experimentation in H14

For this second demonstration, odometry had been integrated and the movements of the rovers were smoother than before.

7   Conclusion and Future Work

We all know that going from a theoretical framework to real life is a major issue. We have not escaped the rule. Starting from a scenario intended to be an illustration of a fundamental problem, we began making it a real world system.

It quickly appeared that to experiment some of the major issues a simulation was required. We then developed one using Unity which proved to be a nice tool both to validate our algorithms and to show what our project would look like once really operational.

Then we moved to real life experimentation. It would be too long to tell about all the issues that we encountered but we have selected the most significant:

- communication: even though the architecture of the system relies on P2P proximity communication, we use Wi-Fi and a structured network in the initial phases for debugging and management purpose. For both demos, the network was quite bad and this is an additional issue (which is out of the perimeter of the project itself) we had to take into account.
- vision: the lighting of the locations and its variability made it really hard to rely on camera only.

- movements: it quickly appeared that odometry was mandatory to have smooth movements of the rovers. Additionally the floor was slippy and made things even worse. We had to adapt to these conditions.
- preparation of the experimentation area: we all know that preparing experimentation fields is time consuming. Once again we did not escape the rule. Installing the nets, sticking the codes on the floor, securing the area, organizing to be able to recharge the batteries during the demonstration, etc. took a significant amount of time. Additionally, preparation is most of the time achieved short before the demonstration, and in this precise case it was the night before, which added to the stress of the operation.

To conclude, these first phases have all been time consuming but the retex we gained will without doubt be useful in the experimentations to come. Additionally it is always a great satisfaction to see a theoretical system come to life!

Thanks

Special thanks to *Bordeaux Metropole* for supporting this work and especially the H14 demonstration. Thanks to the Computer Science Master students of the University of Bordeaux for their involvement in the development of simulations and in the experimentations (both at LaBRI and at H14).

References

1. Px4 official web site. https://px4.io/
2. Aulinas, J., Petillot, Y., Salvi, J., Llado, X.: The Slam Problem: A Survey, vol. 184, pp. 363–371 (2008). https://doi.org/10.3233/978-1-58603-925-7-363
3. Autefage, V., Casteler, A., Chaumette, S., Daguisé, N., Dutartre, A., Mehamli, T.: ParCS-S2: park cleaning swarm supervision system - position paper. In: Proceedings of the 9th AIRTEC International Congress, AIRTEC 2014, Franfurt, Germany, October (2014). https://hal.archives-ouvertes.fr/hal-01115661
4. Autefage, V., Chaumette, S., Magoni, D.: A mission-oriented service discovery mechanism for highly dynamic autonomous swarms of unmanned systems. In: Proceedings of the 12th IEEE International Conference on Autonomic Computing, IEEE ICAC 2015, Grenoble, France, July, pp. 31–40 (2015)
5. Autefage, V., Chaumette, S., Magoni, D.: Comparison of time synchronization techniques in a distributed collaborative swarm system. In: Proceedings of the 24th European Conference on Networks and Communications, EuCNC 2015, Paris, France, June, pp. 460–464. IEEE (2015)
6. Bresson, G., Alsayed, Z., Yu, L., Glaser, S.: Simultaneous localization and mapping: a survey of current trends in autonomous driving. IEEE Trans. Intell. Veh. **2** (2017). https://doi.org/10.1109/TIV.2017.2749181. https://hal.archives-ouvertes. fr/hal-01615897
7. Camp, T., Boleng, J., Davies, V.: A survey of mobility models for ad hoc network research. Wirel. Commun. Mob. Comput. **2**(5), 483–502 (2002)
8. Chaumette, S.: A swarm of drones is more than the sum of the drones that make it up. In: Conference on Complex Systems, CCS 2016, Amsterdam, Netherlands, September (2016). https://hal.archives-ouvertes.fr/hal-01391809

9. Chaumette, S.: Failure is the nominal operation mode for swarms (of drones): reasons and consequences. In: Conference on Complex Systems, CCS 2016. Satellite Session - Swarming Systems: Analysis, Modeling & Design, Amsterdam, Netherlands, September 2016. https://hal.archives-ouvertes.fr/hal-01391810

10. Chaumette, S., Laplace, R., Mazel, C., Godin, A.: Secure cooperative ad hoc applications within UAV fleets - position paper. In: 28th IEEE Military Communications Conference, MILCOM 2009, Boston, United States, October, pp. 1–7 (2009). https://hal.archives-ouvertes.fr/hal-00406478

11. Department of Defense, Washington: Office of the Secretary of Defense: Unmanned aerial vehicle roadmap 2000–2025 (2001)

12. Hoebeke, J., Moerman, I., Dhoedt, B., Demeester, P.: Analysis of decentralized resource and service discovery mechanisms in wireless multi-hop networks. In: Braun, T., Carle, G., Koucheryavy, Y., Tsaoussidis, V. (eds.) WWIC 2005. LNCS, vol. 3510, pp. 181–191. Springer, Heidelberg (2005). https://doi.org/10.1007/11424505_18

13. Hidalgo-Carrió, J., Hennes, D., Schwendner, J., Kirchner, F.: Gaussian process estimation of odometry errors for localization and mapping. In: IEEE International Conference on Robotics and Automation, pp. 5696–5701 (2017)

14. Jazar, R.: Vehicle Dynamics: Theory and Application, pp. 960–988. Springer, Cham (2017). https://doi.org/10.1007/978-3-319-53441-1

15. Kaehler, A., Bradski, G.: Learning OpenCV 3: Computer Vision in C++ with the OpenCV Library. O'Reilly Media, Inc., Sebastopol (2016)

16. Lintrami, T.: Unity 2017 Game Development Essentials, pp. 649–672. Packt Publishing, Birmingham (2018)

17. Quigley, M.: Programming Robots with ROS: A Practical Introduction to the Robot Operating System, pp. 421–432. O'Reilly Media, Sebastopol (2016)

18. Ravikiran, G., Singh, S.: Influence of mobility models on the performance of routing protocols in ad-hoc wireless networks. In: IEEE 59th Vehicular Technology Conference (VTC), May, vol. 4, pp. 2185–2189 (2004)

19. Su, J., Guo, W.: A survey of service discovery protocols for mobile ad hoc networks. In: International Conference on Communications, Circuits and Systems, ICCCAS, May, pp. 398–404 (2008)

20. Wang, R., Wang, J.: Fault diagnosis for four-wheel independently driven electric ground vehicles. IEEE Trans. Veh. Technol. $60(9)$, 4276–4287 (2011)

DroneBallCup: When Drones
Play Volleyball
- First Implementation -

Serge Chaumette[✉] and Matthias Paulmier

Univ. Bordeaux, Bordeaux INP, CNRS, LaBRI, UMR5800, 33400 Talence, France
serge.chaumette@labri.fr
https://www.labri.fr/

Abstract. The ground robots community has setup a competition called the RoboCup [10] (Autonomous Robotics World Cup) to challenge the progress of the technology achieved by both the academy and the industry around a use case that consists in playing football. In this paper we describe a similar approach that we are setting up for autonomous aerial vehicles (drones). The use case is Volleyball.

Keywords: UAV · RPAS · Drones · Autonomous systems · Swarms · Collaboration · Resilience · Computer vision · DroneBallCup · RoboCup

1 Introduction

Aerial drones are complex systems that take advantage of several fields of expertise (aerodynamics, mechanics, computer science, electronics, etc. . .). Today, thanks to the involvement of numerous actors in the academy, the industry and the institutions, a large range of commercial applications are effective. In September 2017, the DGAC[1] [2], which is the French equivalent of the FAA[2] [4], reported several thousands of companies working around drones and, in August of the same year, it had delivered more than 600 licenses to design and build industrial drones.

Despite this very dynamic ecosystem, a significant number of issues still remain unsolved. Their resolution will open more domains of application and new markets. These issues are studied by the researchers/practitioners from both the academy and the industry, often backed up by public institutions.

To support and contribute to the development of the domain, we are currently setting up a competition called DroneBallCup, where drones will play Volleyball (as well as NetBall in the long term). This is based on the model of the RoboCup, as described bellow.

---

[1] *Direction Générale de l'Aviation Civile.*

[2] Federal Aviation Administration.

© Springer Nature Switzerland AG 2019
B. Hilt et al. (Eds.): Nets4Cars/Nets4Trains/Nets4Aircraft 2019, LNCS 11461, pp. 98–108, 2019.
https://doi.org/10.1007/978-3-030-25529-9_9

2 DroneBallCup, a Child Challenge of the RoboCup

Our goal is to bring drones playing Volleyball to the edition of the RoboCup [10] (Autonomous Robotics World Cup) which will be held in Bordeaux, France, in 2020. Our goal for the initial phase, prior to the 2020 edition, is to create a first demonstration that will be presented during the 2019 RoboCup in Sidney, Australia (Fig. 1).

Fig. 1. The DroneBallCup project

2.1 The RoboCup

The following text (courtesy of *Comité RoboCup France* [18]) describes the history and goals of the RoboCup:

> *For more than 20 years, the RoboCup has been a major scientific and technological event. Hosting every year thousands of roboticians from around the world, it is the world's largest robotics and artificial intelligence competition. It was proposed in 1996, by Kitano [10], to stimu-*late research in robotics through a historic challenge: to develop a team of fully autonomous robots able to defeat the soccer world champion human team. *Since then, the RoboCup has developed beyond the challenge strictly related to football: it also includes support for the person or the exploration of disaster sites. Today the event covers all major scientific and technological issues of autonomous robotics.*

From this description it is clear that the ultimate goal of the RoboCup is not to play Football but is to stimulate research on the various topics of autonomous robotics (Fig. 2). Football provides a use case where the most recent breakthroughs can be experimented and the different research groups (from both the academy and the industry) can challenge each other.

Fig. 2. The RoboCup in Eindhoven, 2013 Source: https://www.robocup.fr/, courtesy of *Comité RoboCup France*

2.2   The DroneBallCup

The idea that gave birth to the DroneBallCup is similar to the one that gave birth to the RoboCup. Even though there are many challenges that need to be addressed to make autonomous drones a widely deployed reality in the real world, there is today no real unique challenge that can be used as a reference use case to push research and to confront advances in the field.

It should be noted that the approach that consists in addressing given, hard to solve, use cases has been adopted in several other domains; the reader is for instance referred to the so called Grant Challenges in the domains of High Performance Computing. Some of these challenges have been identified years ago and still push the research forward.

Applying the same philosophy, the DroneBallCup will support and foster the resolution of the issues of the domain of drones (see bellow). To channel the efforts we will set multiple objectives, with increasing complexity from year to year. By doing so, the DroneballCup will give birth to a vibrant environment that will naturally create incentive in the academic and industrial communities and encourage the definition of new partnerships to address the key issues. Like the RoboCup, it will also be a great opportunity for teams to expose and share the progress of their research and the different solutions they have come up with at a national and international level. Finally, the DroneBallCup competition should be an excellent environment for promoting the development of industrial drone products.

3   The Scientific Issues Underlying the DroneBallCup

Here is a non exhaustive list of domains/issues that we have identified and that we believe can be evaluated by *practicing* the sports mentioned above (VolleyBall as a first step and then Netball):

- Management of dynamic environments with moving objects and obstacles
- Flight dynamics
- Autonomous flight
- Collaboration
- Vision and image processing
- Sense and avoid
- Safety and security
- Geo-fencing
- (Distributed) Decision making
- Localization
- Sensor data management
- ...

This list is open, and contributions are more than welcome.

4   DroneBallCup Bordeaux Team

The project is currently funded by *Région Nouvelle Aquitaine*, the University of Bordeaux, LaBRI (Bordeaux Computer Science Research Laboratory), and the other participating Universities and research laboratories (see below). It is also supported by the drones cluster and by the robotics clusters of *Région Nouvelle Aquitaine*. The scientific partners of the project and the specific issues they address are the following (in no particular order):

1. Mechanics and control [19]
   supervisors: Olivier Ly and Hugo Gimbert
   LaBRI, University of Bordeaux
2. Localization [12,17]
   supervisors: Sylvain Marchand and Myriam Desainte-Catherine
   L3i, University of La Rochelle and LaBRI, University of Bordeaux
3. Vision and images
   supervisor: Pascal Desbarats
   LaBRI, University of Bordeaux [15]
4. Sense and avoid [16]
   supervisor: Pierre Melchior
   IMS, University of Bordeaux
5. Swarming, collaboration, cooperation [13][14]
   supervisor: Serge Chaumette
   LaBRI, University of Bordeaux

6. Authority sharing [1]
   supervisor: Damien Sauveron
   XLIM, University of Limoges

This group will of course be happy to welcome[3] any additional contributor willing to get involved in the challenge.

It should be noted that research groups at the University of Le Havre (France) and University of Luxembourg (Luxembourg) are considering setting up similar teams to be able to compete in Bordeaux in 2020.

5   A Pre-step to a Demonstrator: Simulation

A simulation (see Fig. 3) in `python` using `matplolib` [7] as a front end is being developed. This simulation serves as an initial proof of concept for the Volleyball scenario, and makes it possible (and simpler) to explore the numerous issues of making drones play this sport in the real life. It is a setup in which we can experiment our algorithms in a safe environment.

For now, the simulation addresses a limited number of issues. First of all, we have decided to work on the position of the ball, which is the keystone of the system, all other operations depending on it. To determine this position we interpolate its velocity and its acceleration when it is hit by a drone. Then, an algorithm making the drone move to the estimated position of the ball (the issue of keeping the drone on its side of the court is not yet considered) has been implemented. The next step will be to try to shoot the ball in a desired direction and finally to work out if the ball was hit or missed.

Once all of the above problems have been solved, we will work on a more complex scenario with an opponent and a delimited court (the court is not yet taken into account in the simulation).

6   Strategy and Technical Considerations for Building the First Physical Demonstrator

In this section, we explain how we intend to address the first physical demonstrator. It will of course have restricted features, the initial goal being to show that making drones play Volleyball is really feasible. This demonstrator will be a scaled down version of what we expect the DroneBallCup will be in the years to come. For instance, the ball itself will initially be bright red for easy detection and will be partly inflated with helium to make it light enough so that the drones can shoot (push) it easily. In the long term, the ball should be the same as used by human teams (with an increment each year).

---

[3] Point of contact: Serge Chaumette, LaBRI, University of Bordeaux
serge.chaumette@labri.fr.

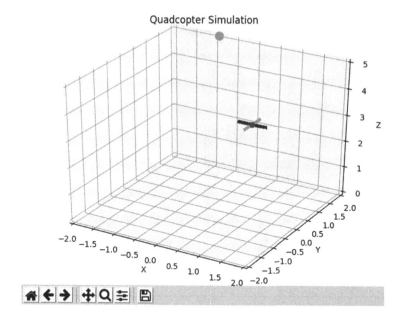

Fig. 3. Visualization of the simulation results

6.1 Court Characteristics

The first demonstrator will show a degraded Volleyball scenario with only two drones (one on each side of the court). As in real Volleyball, a net will be installed at the center of the court to define the different playing zones. The dimensions of the court will be limited for this version as we will use small quadcopters. Each drone will have to defend its side by returning the ball to the other side. Initially, the adversaries will be *friendly* with each other, not trying to win points, but just to send back the ball.

6.2 Centralized System *v.s* Embedded Intelligence

Even though the ultimate goal is to have drones that play in a totally autonomous manner (*i.e.* without instrumenting the court), the first prototype will take advantage of an external system (see Fig. 4) that will be in charge of image processing, ball detection, localization and computation of the trajectories of the drones. Doing so, we free ourselves from the complex task of embedding all the intelligence of the system inside the drones, which is not only difficult because of the small footprint of the aerial platforms that we have chosen (see below), but also because of the low quality sensors that it embeds.

We thus rely on a en external sensor, and for this prototype we have chosen to use a **Kinect** [6] by **Microsoft**. It is a very powerful piece of hardware that offers an RGB camera as well as depth sensors, which is exactly what we need.

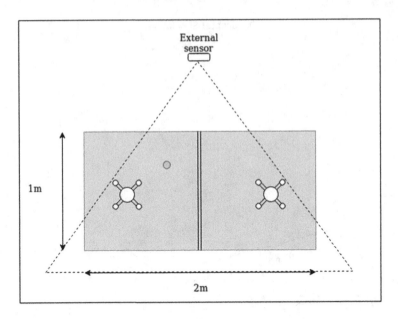

Fig. 4. Physical setup of the first demonstrator

Additionally, software development using this platform is made easy thanks to the `freenect` [11] library and to `OpenCV` [8].

6.3 Aerial Platform

For this first prototype we have selected **CrazyFlies** [5] nano drones (see Fig. 5a). **CrazyFlies** are nano quadrotors built by the **Bitcraze** company. They are readily available and easy to customize. **CrazyFlies** come with an API to control them by writing dedicated programs, and wrappers for several languages are available. The drawback of using this type of hardware is that they are very small and thus only support light payloads (at most 15 g). Still, this remains manageable: when we will switch to a decentralized system with embedded intelligence, the very light Pi Camera v2 (3 g) will be used as the main sensor. This will leave room for a 3D printed structure, which is required for the drone to be able to safely hit the ball. This structure will most likely be a cage with a flat platform at the top, like the one of the DJI Tello (Fig. 5b). This flat platform will make it possible for the drone (at least in the initial phase) to *wait for* the arrival of the ball and then to shoot it (this will free us from complex angles computation).

(a) The crazyflie nano quadcopter   (b) A cage for the DJI Tello

Source: **Source:**

bitcraze.io/crazyflie-2-1/   pgy-tech.com/protective-cage-for-tello/

Fig. 5. Aerial platform selected for the first demonstrator

7   The Major Initial Issue: Precise Localization and Trajectories

To be able to demonstrate a first prototype, the major (even though not the only) issue we have to solve is how to get precise locations. The issue of localization is threefold. It concerns:

- the drones. Each drone must know where it is and where the other drones are.
- the ball. The ball must be localized so that each drone (and the collaborative team of drones as a whole) can decide on a strategy and consequently on a direction where to go.
- the court. This includes the net and the limits of the court.

In the simulation described above (see Sect. 5), we have, by construction, the exact location of the ball and of each drone. It is thus easy to compute the trajectory of the ball (*i.e.* its successive positions) since it follows a perfectly predictable path (assuming we do not have perturbations induced by the environment). In the real world, the sensors are not able to provide precise enough measurements. A Kalman Filter [9] must thus be used to gain more precision.

The strength of the Kalman Filter is that it only needs to remember the previous state of the system and the previous estimate it computed (Fig. 6). Its memory complexity is thus very low. It is also a very fast way to get a good approximation of the state (position and velocity) of an object without having to rely on expensive accurate sensors.

There are two main processes at work in a Kalman Filter. First, the `predict` function takes the current state of the considered object and estimates its new state. This function also updates a **covariance matrix** which gives the error in the estimate knowing the previous estimate and measurement. The `update` function then additionally updates the state of the target object as estimated previously, taking into account the prediction (computed by the `predict` function) and measurement (collected via a sensor), respectively weighted by the

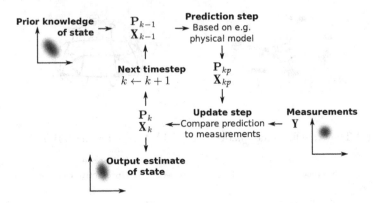

Fig. 6. Basic concept of Kalman Filtering. Based on: upload.wikimedia.org/wikipedia/commons/a/a5/Basic_concept_of_Kalman_filtering.svg

P and H matrices (see below). In a 3D situation where we want to take into account the position and the velocity of the considered object, the state X at iteration k is a 6×1 matrix containing the x, y and z positions of the drone as well as its velocity in each direction:

$$X_k = \begin{bmatrix} x_k \\ y_k \\ z_k \\ \dot{x}_k \\ \dot{y}_k \\ \dot{z}_k \end{bmatrix}$$

The prediction process updates the predicted state (the index denotes the prediction (p) values, i.e. kp is an intermediate estimated state)

$$X_{kp} = AX_{k-1} + Bu_k + w_k$$

and the predicted covariance

$$P_{kp} = AP_{k-1}A^T + Q_k$$

P is the state covariance matrix and u represents the model of the physical system. In our case u is a 3×1 matrix containing the forces applied when the ball hits another object (a drone or the floor). It also takes gravity into account. Q is the process (or prediction) noise covariance matrix. It represents the error that can occur in the prediction. This matrix prevents P from going down to 0 making the prediction weight too much compared to the weight of the real measurement. As any noise covariance matrix [3] Q is hard to determine and is mostly found empirically. We will thus need to run a large number of experiments to evaluate it. w is a noise factor that is set to 0 in this scenario because the drones will play in the absence of external noise (no wind, no communication perturbations, etc. . .)

A and B are matrices that allow to integrate time into the equations to compute accelerations and velocities.

The update process is as follows:

$$K_p = \frac{P_{kp}H}{HP_{kp}H^T + R}$$

$$X_k = X_{kp} + K[Y - HX_{kp}]$$

K is the Kalman gain, a matrix that represents the weight given to the measurement and state estimate. H is the observation model. It allows to match the observed and predicted values into the space in which the object is moving (performing rotations and translations). R is the measurement noise covariance matrix. Y is the measured value.

We finally update the P matrix:

$$P_k = (I - KH)P_{kp}$$

to allow the Kalman filter to take into account the computed error in the estimate for the next iteration.

8   Perspectives

In this paper, we have presented the DroneBallCup, a competition that we are setting up to foster research on drones by making it possible to demonstrate on a yearly basis the progress accomplished by the researchers/practitioners. This competition is a *pretext* to address the multiple yet unresolved or partly resolved issues of the domain, and to compare and share results obtained by the contributors. To our knowledge, there is no other initiative of this kind.

We have also presented our work on an initial demonstrator that we are developing using CrazyFlies nano drones.

Finally, we believe that a Volleyball and (if time allows) a Netball competition with drones as players would certainly be a plus for the 2020 RoboCup in Bordeaux. The plan is to build a first demonstrator to be shown at the 2019 RoboCup in Sidney in order to motivate the potential creation of teams and to eventually create a full league[4] for 2020.

---

[4] A league in the RoboCup in a specific competition/challenge with its own characteristics and constraints.

References

1. Akram, R.N., et al.: Security, privacy and safety evaluation of dynamic and static fleets of drones. In: 2017 IEEE/AIAA 36th Digital Avionics Systems Conference (DASC), pp. 1–12. IEEE (2017)
2. DGAC - official web site. https://www.ecologique-solidaire.gouv.fr/direction-generale-laviation-civile-dgac/
3. Duník, J., Šimandl, M., Straka, O.: Methods for estimating state and measurement noise covariance matrices: aspects and comparison. IFAC Proc. Vol. 42(10), 372–377 (2009)
4. FAA - official web site. https://www.faa.gov/
5. Giernacki, W., Skwierczyński, M., Witwicki, W., Wroński, P., Kozierski, P.: Crazyflie 2.0 quadrotor as a platform for research and education in robotics and control engineering. In: 2017 22nd International Conference on Methods and Models in Automation and Robotics (MMAR), pp. 37–42. IEEE (2017)
6. Han, J., Shao, L., Xu, D., Shotton, J.: Enhanced computer vision with microsoft kinect sensor: a review. IEEE Trans. Cybern. 43(5), 1318–1334 (2013)
7. Hunter, J.D.: Matplotlib: a 2D graphics environment. Comput. Sci. Eng. 9(3), 90 (2007)
8. Kaehler, A., Bradski, G.: Learning OpenCV 3: Computer Vision in C++ with the OpenCV Library. O'Reilly Media, Inc., Newton (2016)
9. Kalman, R.E.: A new approach to linear filtering and prediction problems. J. Basic Eng. 82(1), 35–45 (1960)
10. Kitano, H., Asada, M.: The robocup humanoid challenge as the millennium challenge for advanced robotics. Adv. Robot. 13(8), 723–736 (1998)
11. The libfreenect project page. https://openkinect.org/wiki/Main_Page
12. Mouba Ndjila, J.: Manipulations spatiales de sons spectraux. Ph.D. thesis, Université de Bordeaux 1 (2009). http://www.theses.fr/2009BOR13869
13. Namuduri, K., Chaumette, S., Kim, J.H., Sterbenz, J.P.: UAV Networks and Communications. Cambridge University Press, Cambridge (2017)
14. Chaumette, S.: Cooperating UAVs and swarming. In: UAV Networks and Communications. Cambridge University Press (2017)
15. Oleynikova, H., Honegger, D., Pollefeys, M.: Reactive avoidance using embedded stereo vision for mav flight. In: 2015 IEEE International Conference on Robotics and Automation (ICRA), pp. 50–56. IEEE (2015)
16. Poty, A.: Planification de trajectoire dans un environnement dynamique et génération de mouvement d'ordre non entier. Ph.D. thesis, Université de Bordeaux 1 (2006). http://www.theses.fr/2006BOR13202
17. Pulkki, V.: Virtual sound source positioning using vector base amplitude panning. J. Audio Eng. Soc. 45(6), 456–466 (1997)
18. Official web site of Comité RoboCup France. https://robocup.fr/
19. Rouxel, Q., Passault, G., Hofer, L., N'Guyen, S., Ly, O.: Learning the odometry on a small humanoid robot. In: 2016 IEEE International Conference on Robotics and Automation (ICRA), pp. 1810–1816. IEEE (2016)

Rail

Hardware-in-the-Loop and Software-in-the-Loop Platform for Testing and Validation of Adaptable Radio Communications Systems for Railways at IP Layer

Juan Moreno[1], Maha Bouaziz[2(✉)], Marion Berbineau[2], Ying Yan[3],
José Soler[3], Raul Torrego[4], Val Iñaki[4], Alessandro Vizzarri[5],
Laurent Clavier[6], Rédha Kassi[6], Yann Cocheril[2], Virginie Deniau[2],
and Christophe Gransart[2]

[1] Área de Ingeniería, Metro de Madrid S.A., Madrid, Spain
juan.moreno@metromadrid.es
[2] University Lille Nord de France, IFSTTAR, COSYS, LEOST,
59650 Villeneuve d'Ascq, France
maha_bouaziz@yahooo.fr
[3] DTU Fotonik, Technical University of Denmark, 2800 Kgs. Lyngby, Denmark
[4] IK4-Ikerlan Technology Research Centre, 20500 Arrasate-Mondragon, Spain
[5] Radiolabs, Consorzio Università Industria Laboratori Di Radiocomunicazioni,
Corso d'Italia 19, 00198 Rome, Italy
[6] Univ. Lille, CNRS, UMR8520 - IEMN, 59000 Lille, France

Abstract. This paper presents a description of a new emulation platform to help decrease expenses for the development of a new train-to-ground communication system for railways, which is one of the objectives of the Shift2Rail Joint Undertaking. This emulator will interface with the T2G communication prototypes at IP layer and will consider many railway-specific services, perturbations and physical layer scenarios. It will combine modern approaches for testing like hardware-in-the-loop and software-in-the-loop in order to mimic railways environment and radio access technologies on an efficient way. In this paper we explain all these aspects, beginning with the railway particular circumstances to be taken into account and ending with an explanation of the approach for the development of the emulator.

Keywords: HITL · SITL · OAI · Railways · Train-to-ground communications · Wireless

1 Introduction

Communication systems in railways last very long until they become obsolete but, on the other hand, also take a lot of time until they are developed, fully tested, validated and put into service. The reasons are many but the most important one is the presence of some railway-specific constraints like fragmentation in regulation, technical complexity, safety implications, *etc.* Shift2Rail JU [1], among its multiple objectives, has

© Springer Nature Switzerland AG 2019
B. Hilt et al. (Eds.): Nets4Cars/Nets4Trains/Nets4Aircraft 2019, LNCS 11461, pp. 111–118, 2019.
https://doi.org/10.1007/978-3-030-25529-9_10

the development of a new adaptable train-to-ground (T2G) communications system able to overcome the limitations of the T2G communication systems available in the market, which are restricting the performance and evolution of some railway services for train control and command like ETCS (European Train Control System) and CBTC (Communications-based Train Control). This new T2G system must be developed according to user requirements defined in the X2RAIl-1 project [2] and based on both NGTC [3] and FRMCS [4, 5] specifications. Five key user requirements can be highlighted [2]:

- The system will be adaptable in terms of bearer selection and configuration as required by prevailing QoS demand and availability, and scale in terms of performance, reach and number of users.
- The network will provide a convenient means for migration, upgrade and maintainability, co-existence and backward compatibility when required.
- The network will be able to support safety-critical communication for railway applications, and be able to provide connectivity to selected third party users, such as primary emergency services.
- The system will be resilient to service disruption, for example, through equipment failure, malicious events, or interference.
- The system requirements should allow for the design of a system that lowers energy and environmental impacts when compared to existing solutions.

To avoid a costly and fragmented validation process including on site testing for this new adaptable T2G communication, the European Emulradio4rail Project [6] will provide an innovative emulation platform for tests and validation of various radio access technologies (RAT) like Wi-Fi, LTE, LTE-A, 5G and Satellites. The platform will combine simulations of the communication core network and emulation of various RAT thanks to the coupling of discrete event simulator such as RIVERBED Modeler (former OPNET Modeler) [7], Open Air Interface (OAI) [8], several radio channel emulators, models of IP parameters and real physical systems.

The project is an open call project in the Innovation Program 2 of Shift2Rail. It is led by IFSTTAR with the participation of IKERLAN, DTU, Eurnex, RadioLabs, University of Lille and Metro de Madrid. The emulation platform will interface with different industrial prototypes of the new adaptable communication system at IP layer under development in the X2RAIl-3 project [9]. The testing scenarios will take into account many different railway-related services like ERTMS or CBTC, the influence of real environments based on radio channel emulation at Physical layer and also common perturbations present in railway scenarios (impulsive noises, potential jammers, etc.). Parts of the emulation platforms will take into account previous works done to evaluate railway communications in different context [10, 11].

The structure of this article is as follows: Sect. 2 provides an overview of the different requirements for the emulation platform; in Sect. 3 the technical alternatives and the development process are explained and, finally, in Sect. 4 conclusions are drawn.

2   Requirements for the Emulation Tool

In this section we will explain the requirements for the emulation tool in three different categories: the Key Performance Indicators (KPI) that will perceive the railway services, the railway scenarios to be considered (this is, the channel models available in the literature that will be emulated using hardware channel emulators) and the potential perturbations to be injected. In Fig. 1 a general schematic of the architecture of the emulation platform is shown. PLMN stands for Public Land Mobile Network and SITL means System-In-The-Loop (SITL). The SITL module is a Riverbed module that interfaces simulations with real systems. It provides an interface for connecting live network hardware or software applications to a Riverbed discrete event simulation.

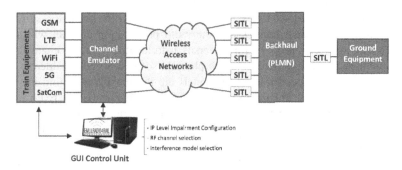

Fig. 1. Block diagram of the proposed emulation platform.

2.1   Services and Radio Access Technologies

In railways, there are many different services and they are usually divided into three different categories: safety-critical, operator-oriented and passenger-oriented [2]. In the first type, we find transmission-based signaling systems like ETCS and CBTC, radiotelephony and few more. The requirements are significant in terms of reliability and robustness but not demanding in terms of throughput. In the second type, we find non-critical services that provide added-value to operators, like remote maintenance, condition-based maintenance systems, real-time video surveillance (Close Circuit TeleVision), and a large etcetera. The throughput needs to be high and both the delay and jitter delay need to be low. Finally, services for customers include WiFi access to the Internet, passenger information, *etc.*, which are non-critical at all and usually demand a very large capacity to the communication links. Coming from both new standards like 5G and the increased competitiveness from other transportation systems, many more services are coming in the future [12].

The Adaptable Communication System (ACS) prototypes for all railways under development in X2RAIL-3 project will be "technology independent". This means that several bearers will coexist in parallel, for example LTE and Wi-Fi and satellite communications. The ACS will be capable to select the suitable radio access network based on application requirements, user equipment coverage, traffic profile in the areas, *etc*. Therefore, the Emulradio4rail platform will have to consider many RATs: IEEE 802.11, 3GPP LTE, future 5G New Radio (5G NR) and satellite communications (SatComs) as it is illustrated in Fig. 1.

2.2   Railway Scenarios

The word "railways" could be misleading because it covers a large array of scenarios like high-speed, mainline, regional, intercity, metro, tramway and, on a more general point of view, other related technologies which do not have rail-wheel contact like MagLev. Four main railway operating scenarios are considered in Shift2Rail: mainline, metro/urban, regional, freight.

In the aforementioned scenarios, rolling stock, speed, track geometry, surrounding environment differs, which implies that the radio propagation channel will differ as well. The way to address properly this diversity is to identify the radio channel models already published that fit better with each physical scenario to be considered.

In particular, high-speed trains and tunnels are the most challenging in terms of complexity and potential impact on the radio channel characteristics. Even when we consider tunnels, the propagation characteristics differ significantly depending on the shape, presence of curves, wall materials, *etc*. For example in [13] the authors present several challenges for wireless communications for the high-speed rail context. [14] presents a survey on channel measurements and models for high-speed train communication systems in the case of T2G. [15] proposes a Winner model in tunnels at 5.8 GHz for WiFi like systems. [16] highlights phenomena like keyholes which make Multiple Input Multiple Output (MIMO) diversity useless in tunnels under certain conditions. In Fig. 2 some examples of railway environments are shown. High-speed lines are commonly assumed to be a rural scenario but, in fact, it is very frequent to go through cuttings, viaducts and tunnels whose propagation conditions differ in a significant way. In addition to the various geographical scenarios, it is important to mention that the radio channel model could be different for each RAT depending on frequency bands and bandwidth.

The wireless channel can be modeled inside an FPGA with a simple model known as the tapped delay line (TDL) [17]:

$$h(t, \tau) = \sum_{n=1}^{N} r_n(t) e^{-j\Phi_n(t, \tau_n(t))} \delta(t, \tau_n(t)) \tag{1}$$

where $h(t,\tau)$ represents the time-variant complex impulse response to the input signal $r_n(t,\tau_n(t))$. As can be observed in Fig. 3, each tap is the product of the complex baseband signal and a complex coefficient, which modifies the amplitude and phase signal together with the addition of a delay.

Fig. 2. Examples of different railway environments

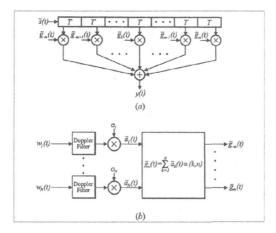

Fig. 3. Uniformly spaced TDL model for discrete multipath channel. (a) TDL structure; (b) generation of tap-gain processes: input processes are independent, zero-mean Gaussian processes [18].

2.3 Perturbations

The radio channel emulation will have to take into account the main representative potential sources of degradation in the radio channel that could affect the overall performance. In general terms, there are two potential sources of degradation: non-intentional and intentional interferences. Examples of non-intentional interferences are interferences from public mobile operators using adjacent frequency bands, electric arcs formed in the imperfect pantograph-catenary contact [19], network overloads, *etc*. Among the intentional perturbations, we can consider also electromagnetic attacks with various types of jammers [20]. All these perturbations that could be found in the literature review need to be modelled and taken into account in the emulation platform in addition to the channel model.

Interference models have been widely used but essentially for receiver design or global network performance evaluation. They have been less applied in emulation environment; in particular the real time implementation, as well as the dependence structure (their dynamicity), are not so well studied. Besides, intentional interferences are also less known. Finally, they could necessitate some specific indicators, the traditional signal to noise radio not being a sufficient statistics, because it ignores its impulsive characteristic. The impact on the RAT may vary (for example, GSM-R does not implement MIMO techniques; and the resilience against interference varies significantly if the waveform is narrowband or wideband).

3   Emulation Platform

The need for emulation of realistic radio environment conditions to test wireless communication systems is increasing for industry and transport applications where automation required deployment of various wireless communications [11, 21]. Emulradio4rail project will go a step further. The novelty proposed here is to consider coupling between RIVERBED Modeler and Open Air Interface (OAI) instead of considering classical network emulator. This solution will improve the Hardware/Software co-simulation platform with integration of a radio channel emulator as illustrated in Fig. 1. Using OAI network emulator reduces the cost of real equipment for establishing LTE network for example.

Riverbed Modeler is a discrete-event simulation tool used for the network modelling and performance evaluation. It supports various network types and technologies allowing to design and study communication networks, devices, protocols and applications. This simulator is a graphical-based editor that makes it easy to use for network components structure. Using RIVERBED Modeler provides abilities to simulate various network entities and analyse performances by models. The RIVERBED Modeler network simulator is deployed to provide capabilities to traffic monitoring and simulation of the trackside RATs. The co-simulation software modules capture the real LTE traffic from the LTE EPC, process the traffic in the simulation environment and forward the traffic to the application servers in the real environment. In such a way, it is possible to emulate the impact of different concurrent traffic types within the core network and assess the impact on the target traffic/application under test.

OAI is an open-source hardware and software wireless technology platform created for research tasks and used for simulation, emulation and real-time execution of 3GPP cellular networks. The main advantages of OAI is its high level of realism. OAI is a Software Defined Radio (SDR) based solution and provides a complete software implementation of all elements of the 4G LTE system architecture. The methodology deployed in the OAI platform is to use the real protocol stack to perform more realistic and reliable emulations. Regarding the configurations for an in-lab radio network experiment, the OAI installs the software platform on the host computer and runs the full protocol stack in the emulation mode. The proposed eNodeB experimental testbed consists of two elements: RF hardware as the radio part and a computer as the baseband unit. The transceiver functionality is realized using a Software Defined Radio (SDR) card connected to a host computer for processing. Besides, the EPC (Evolved Packet Core) features included in OAI can also be used in order to connect real equipment at IP level. The OAI is currently in evolution towards the future 5G.

The connection between the network emulator (OAI) and the network simulator (Riverbed modeler), a tool called System-In-The-Loop (SITL) provides an interface between a simulated network running in Riverbed Modeler and a real test platform. With SITL, a simulation environment can connect and interact with the external physical hardware in real-time.

The Emulradio4rail project will implement a software/hardware co-simulation model consisting of both physical emulator and software simulation environment. Combining real test environment and simulated network scenario, especially adding the channel emulator into an integrated platform, provides close-to-the-field test results in a lab-scale testbed. In this way, the testbed can offer quite a full-stack (from physical layer to IP level) test environment representative of the various railway environments thanks both to the various radio channel models and interference models implemented in the channel emulator.

4   Conclusions

The Emulradio4rail testing platform presented in this paper aims at proposing innovative solutions to drastically reduce the costs and burden of testing and validation procedures of the T2G adaptable communication systems with various RATs. This tool will increase accessibility to testing solutions in Europe and will reduce time-to-market for radio access technologies. The platform will permit reproducibility of tests with zero on site testing. We have seen the complexity of the task to be achieved due to the necessity to emulate a significant diversity of railway scenarios, services and potential perturbations. We have explained the detailed requirements in terms of these three aspects and the general approach for the development of the emulation platform, which will interface at IP layer with the T2G adaptable communications prototypes that will be provided by industry within the framework of X2RAIL-3 project.

References

1. Available on: https://shift2rail.org/
2. X2RAIL-1 D3.1 - User & System Requirements (Telecommunications) – available for download on http://projects.shift2rail.org/s2r_ip2_n.aspx?p=X2RAIL-1
3. NGTC: D6.1_Requirements_Specifications_for_IPcomm_system_FINAL.pdf. Available for download at http://www.ngtc.eu/results-publications/LNCS Homepage, http://www.springer.com/lncs. Accessed 21 Nov 2016
4. FRMCS requirements - Draft-3GPP-related-FRMCS-S1-171207-TR22.889V0.4.0.-rev
5. FRMCS: Future Rail Mobile Communications System, Available: https://uic.org/frmcs
6. Emulradio4rail: http://www.emulradio4rail.eu. Project: https://projects.shift2rail.org/s2r_ip2_n.aspx?p=EMULRADIO4RAIL

7. Riverbed: RIVERBED MODELER. The fastest discrete event-simulation engine for analyzing and designing communication networks, April 2019. https://www.riverbed.com/dk/products/steelcentral/steelcentral-riverbed-modeler.htmlOpenAirInterface, https://www.openairinterface.org/

8. OpenAirInterface: 5G software alliance for democratising wireless innovation. https://www.openairinterface.org/

9. Allen, B., Eschbach, B., Mikulandra, M.: Defining an adaptable communications system for all railways. In: Proceedings 7th Transport Research Arena TRA 2018 (TRA 2018), Vienna, 16–19 April 2018. https://doi.org/10.5281/zenodo.1456472

10. Bouaziz, M., Yan, Y., Kassab, M., Soler, J., Berbineau, M.: Evaluating TCMS train-to-ground communication performances based on the LTE technology and discrete event simulations. In: 13th International workshop on communication technologies for vehicles (Nets4cars-Nets4trains-Nets4Aircraft-Nets4spacecrafts), May 2018

11. Díez, V., et al.: Validation of an LTE backbone for inter-car communications in metro environments. In: 12th European Conference on Antennas and Propagation (EuCAP 2018), London, pp. 1–5 (2018). https://doi.org/10.1049/cp.2018.0960

12. Moreno, J., Riera, J.M., de Haro, L., Rodriguez, C.: A survey on future railway radio communications services: challenges and opportunities. IEEE Commun. Mag. 53(10), 62–68 (2015). https://doi.org/10.1109/mcom.2015.7295465

13. Wu, J., Fan, P.: A survey on high mobility wireless communications: challenges, opportunities and solutions. IEEE Access 4, 450–476 (2016). https://doi.org/10.1109/ACCESS.2016.2518085

14. Wang, C., Ghazal, A., Ai, B., Liu, Y., Fan, P.: Channel measurements and models for high-speed train communication systems: a survey. IEEE Commun. Surv. Tutor. 18(2), 974–987 (2016). https://doi.org/10.1109/comst.2015.2508442

15. Hairoud, S., Combeau, P., Pousset, Y., Cocheril, Y., Berbineau, M.: WINNER model for subway tunnel at 5.8 GHz. In: 2012 12th International Conference on ITS Telecommunications, Taipei, pp. 743–747 (2012). https://doi.org/10.1109/itst.2012.6425280

16. Moreno, J., de Haro, L., Rodríguez, C., Cuéllar, L., Riera, J.M.: Keyhole estimation of an MIMO-OFDM train-to-wayside communication system on subway tunnels. IEEE Antennas Wirel. Propag. Lett. 14, 88–91 (2015). https://doi.org/10.1109/LAWP.2014.2356076

17. Proakis, J.G., Salehi, M.: Digital Communications. McGraw-Hill, New York (2008)

18. Jeruchim, M.C., Balaban, P., Shanmugan, K.S.: Simulation of communication systems modeling, methodology and techniques. Springer, New York (2006)

19. Hassan, K., Gautier, R., Dayoub, I., Berbineau, M., Radoi, E.: Multiple-antenna-based blind spectrum sensing in the presence of impulsive noise. IEEE Trans. Veh. Technol. 63(5), 2248–2257 (2014). https://doi.org/10.1109/TVT.2013.2290839

20. Deniau, V., Gransart, C., Romero, G.L., Simon, E.P., Farah, J.: IEEE 802.11n communications in the presence of frequency-sweeping interference signals. IEEE Trans. Electromagn. Compat. 59(5), 1625–1633 (2017). https://doi.org/10.1109/TEMC.2017.2684428

21. Schwind, A., Berlt, P., Lorenz, M., Schneider, C., Hein, M.A.: Over-the-air MIMO channel emulation for automotive LTE radio systems using software defined radio. In: 12th European Conference on Antennas and Propagation (EuCAP 2018), London, pp. 1–5 (2018). https://doi.org/10.1049/cp.2018.0399

Author Index

Printed in the United States
By Bookmasters